GREAT QUESTIONS OF THE
LAST WEEK

GREAT QUESTIONS
OF THE LAST WEEK

B. H. BRUNER

COKESBURY PRESS
NASHVILLE - TENNESSEE

DESIGNED, SET UP, ELECTROTYPED, PRINTED, AND
BOUND BY THE PARTHENON PRESS AT NASH-
VILLE, TENNESSEE, UNITED STATES OF AMERICA

C

PREFACE

THE EVENTS of the last week have always been prominent in the thought and life of the Church. Hardly a scene in that week but that has been made immortal by the great artists of the centuries. Many of the greatest hymns of the Church center around the passion of Jesus, and most of the theology of the Church finds its roots there.

Our interest in the pages which follow has to do, not with the great events of the last week as such, but with some of the great questions which were raised during that week. They are questions which go to the very heart of the religion which claims to have its source and inspiration in Jesus of Nazareth. They are questions which the human mind cannot let alone, and which the Church is forced to face in every age. They are questions which touch the conscience and will of mankind as well as its mind.

There is no better time to face these great questions of our faith than during those days which lead up to the last week. Surely that period is no time to deal with the more superficial questions of religion. They are not days in which the purely organizational life of the Church should be stressed and they should never be dedicated to any purely promotional program. The Church has the ear of the people during this period to a greater extent than at any other time in the year. And if the Church would set itself during this period to a restudy of the most vital elements in its faith, and to a clear and candid presentation of them, it would greatly deepen its spiritual life and increase its power and influence among men.

CONTENTS

ACKNOWLEDGMENTS

THE READING AND REREADING of many books has been a part of the preparation of this series of studies, and the thoughts and words of many others are mingled with those of the author. Direct or indirect quotations appear from the following books and magazines: *Aspects of Christ*, W. B. Selbie; *The Religion of Jesus* and *Our Recovery of Jesus*, Walter E. Bundy (Bobbs-Merrill Company); *Things Fundamental*, Charles E. Jefferson (Thomas Y. Crowell Company); *If I Had Only One Sermon to Preach*, American Series (Harper and Brothers); *The Master*, Walter Russell Bowie (Scribners); *The Authority and Person of Our Lord*, John A. Hutton (Fleming H. Revell Company); *The Gospel for an Age of Doubt*, Henry van Dyke; *The Person of Christ*, Philip Schaff (Ray Long and Richard R. Smith Company, Inc.); *Behold the Man*, Friedrich Rittelmeyer (Macmillan Company); *Productive Beliefs*, Lynn Harold Hough (Abingdon Press); *The Gospel of Matthew*, Charles R. Erdman (Westminster Press); *Robertson's Sermons* (Harper and Brothers); *Watching the Cross*, J. D. Jones (Ray Long and Richard R. Smith, Inc.); *Jesus in the Experience of Men*, T. R. Glover (Ray Long and Richard R. Smith, Inc.); *Our City of God*, J. Brierly (Pilgrim Press); *The Call of the Cross*, George D. Herron (Fleming H. Revell Company); *The Christian Century* and *The Christian Evangelist*.

WHO IS JESUS?

"And when he was come into Jerusalem, all the city was stirred, saying, Who is this?"

MATTHEW 21: 10.

I
WHO IS JESUS?

EVERYWHERE Jesus went while he was on earth he caused a stir. His words and deeds so stirred the people to the depths of their minds and souls that they were either whole-heartedly for or against him. There was something about Jesus which made it hard for people to remain neutral in his presence. Jesus was a disturbing factor in Palestine in the first century. The people in the cities and villages which he visited knew that something had happened in their presence. And always, the stir which Jesus created was followed by the question, "Who is this?" Men wanted to know what manner of man Jesus was. Who was this man who spake as never man spake and whose utterances had the unmistakable stamp of authority upon them? Who was this man who was so perfectly at home among the mysteries of God's universe that its laws and forces responded to him in such a way that he was able to do things which no other man had ever done? To what order did he belong? Was he prophet or priest? Was he genuine, or was he a blasphemer and impostor? Did his power come from God or

Satan? Was he man or God? Up and down the highways of Palestine, in the villages of Judea and Galilee, and even in Samaria, the leading question of the day was the question about Jesus. It is not strange, then, that when he entered Jerusalem for the last time the whole city was stirred, and the question upon all lips was, "Who is this?" It was only the culmination of a tide of interest in Jesus which had reached its heights. It was only natural that his entrance into the city should arouse both the minds and the imaginations of the people.

This question about Jesus was answered in Jerusalem during that last week. The multitudes received him as "the prophet Jesus, from Nazareth of Galilee," "the Son of David," and "the King that cometh in the name of the Lord." This was their first answer. Their second answer, when Jesus stood before Pilate, was the answer of utter rejection. The Jewish leaders called Jesus an impostor, a blasphemer, a pretender to the throne of David and a rival of Cæsar, a disturber of the people and a perverter of the nation. In their eyes, he was a man worthy of death. Pilate, the representative of the Roman Empire, found in him a faultless and innocent man, delivered into his presence because of the envy of the Jews, and not worthy of death. In the eyes of at least one of the robbers who hung on a cross beside Jesus, he was a Saviour, and the Roman officer who watched him die confessed that he was "a righteous man" and "the Son of God." The disciples and the other immediate followers of Jesus were strangely silent during that last week, and

16

the words of one of them as he journeyed toward Emmaus, "We hoped that it was he who should redeem Israel," words of deep disappointment, probably reveal what was in the minds of most of them.

For nineteen hundred years this same Jesus has been coming into our comfortable Jerusalems and causing a stir. And whenever he comes the same question is raised—"Who is this?" He came to that group of frightened and discouraged disciples who had left his body in a tomb with the Roman seal upon it, and he did not leave them until they had answered this question. He came to the empire whose representative had given the word to crucify him, and continued to cause a stir until this question was answered. And then, when the Church had taken the place of this empire and through its greed for power had practically excluded Jesus from its life and plunged civilization into the darkness of night, he came again in the Protestant Reformation and demanded that this question be answered again. He came to the eighteenth century with its intellectualism and dawning industrialism and caused such a stir that this question had to be reckoned with. He came to the nineteenth century with its wealth of knowledge, its perfection of representative government, its scientific discoveries, its literary achievements and its religious devotion, and made this question one of the great questions of the century. He has come again in the twentieth century to disturb us.

Jesus has come into the Jerusalem of a divided and bewildered Church in the twentieth century and has stirred it to its very foundations. For years the

17

leaders of institutionalized religion have talked about the need for the recovery of the real Jesus. Now that he has come, with a very few exceptions, they do not know what to do with him. He does not fit into their institutionalism and complacent orthodoxy, and they are greatly disturbed over his ethical and social and even religious demands. The Church is divided because the leaders have ignored the fact that Jesus is its only head; it is bewildered because, in the presence of many ways and in the midst of many voices, it has tried almost every way except the way of Jesus and has failed to listen to the one voice which has the word of life. The most insistent question in the modern Church, the question which comes up at every turn and which is crowding all other questions into the background, is the question about Jesus. Jesus will continue to disturb the Church which wears his name until this question is answered adequately for the twentieth century. This answer may not be a new answer; but the Church must find it and declare it in a language which can be understood by this century if it is to maintain its religious leadership among men.

Jesus has come into the Jerusalem of our social and industrial order which, for the most part, has been built by men who have professed to be his followers, and he has caused a tremendous stir. These men who have built our civilization upon the foundations of force, the acquisitive instinct, the policy of enlightened self-interest and unlimited competition, are being greatly disturbed by a Jesus who, they thought, was safely imprisoned in the creeds and dogmas of ortho-

18

dox religion. When he has stepped out of those creeds and dogmas as a living personality and confronted these men as the friend of the oppressed and the enemy of the oppressor; when he has put the value of a child of God and an eternal soul upon each human individual, and by declaring that this individual is the most valuable thing in the world shattering with one single blow the fundamental principle of modern industry that machines and profits are of more value than men; when he repudiates that beautiful and comfortable doctrine of the rich that heaven is a place somewhere in the skies where all the inequalities of earth will be made up for, and proceeds to outline a program for the kingdom of heaven on earth in which men shall live as brothers and equals in a co-operative rather than a competitive society; when he puts the emphasis upon justice rather than charity and would substitute love for force—they want to know who he is. Who is this Jesus who makes such searching demands upon our modern life? Be sure that the leaders of our present order will not listen to his demands until this question is answered.

Jesus has come into the troubled Jerusalem of our international affairs in the twentieth century, and his presence is the source of grave concern on the part of the men who are trying to conduct these affairs. He is causing a stir among the nations to-day. The God of battles—our international leaders know. They have called upon Him many times. The Christ of mercy who has inspired both men and women to minister to the victims of war, they know. They have said

19

many beautiful things about him. But this Jesus who comes to say again, "Put up the sword; he that taketh the sword shall perish by the sword," and "Love your enemies"; this Jesus who insists upon the solidarity of the race and the brotherhood of man as a fact to be acted upon rather than a beautiful sentiment to be written about; this Jesus who calls men to an utter repudiation of force as the final or the best method for settling international differences; this Jesus who would be the Prince of Peace in reality and not in name only—Who is he? The leaders of the nations have kept him out of their peace councils and disarmament conferences. He has had no place in the discussions of the international bankers. But "the doors being shut," he has come to stand in the midst of all councils and conferences to trouble the leaders with his insistent demands for a civilization built upon coöperation and human values rather than competition and profits, and for a warless world and a peace and good will among the nations which rests upon a genuinely Christian foundation. Who is this Jesus? Before the nations take him seriously enough to act upon his demands, this question must be answered in a decisive manner.

Where shall we turn for an adequate answer to the question about Jesus? There are some answers which, no matter how popular they may be in certain circles, will not suffice. The answer of the historic creeds and much of our Christian theology is no longer adequate. The answer of those who believe only in the humanity of Jesus is not sufficient. And the an-

20

swer of those who insist that we do not know, and perhaps never can know, whether Jesus ever lived or not, and that if he should prove to be only a myth it would not greatly alter the ideals of his religion, is no answer at all.

The historic creeds and traditional Christian theology have their answer to the question about Jesus. And in spite of the fact that multitudes of people are no longer taking this answer for granted in their quest for Jesus, it is, perhaps, the most unanimous answer in the Christian world. Undoubtedly in the beginning Christian fact and Christian doctrine were very close together. Something happened in time and space which provided a sufficient basis for doctrine. But under the influence of Greek philosophy, which laid its hands on Christianity very soon after its birth, the gulf between fact and doctrine began to widen. It is quite easy to follow the road by which the ''historical Jesus became the unhistorical Christ'' of the second- and fourth-century theology. We may have a natural development of thought in the formation of creeds, but we do not have a natural development of Christian doctrine from historical data. In the second century the historical element in Jesus' life began to recede into the background, and when we reach the fourth century the portrait of Jesus which we find is definitely unhistorical. In the place of the ''historical Jesus we have a metaphysical Christ, whose humanity was indeed acknowledged in word, but who lacked all the attributes of humanity which we know.'' The historic creeds do not present a total portrait of Jesus. They

21

are defended by those who assume that "the Christian facts involve the whole superstructure of doctrine which has been built upon them, form and substance alike." And because the mind of the twentieth century does not accept this assumption as valid, the answer to the creeds about Jesus is not adequate. These creeds, valuable as they are as historic documents, are to-day a millstone about the neck of many Christians, and a stumblingblock in the way of many outside the Church whose real sympathy is with the religion of Jesus. So long as men have to struggle "and submit to evasions and reservations in order to accept them," they will become the means of "stultifying the whole intellectual position of those who use them."

And because much of our traditional Christian theology starts from the position of the creeds, its answer to the question about Jesus is unsatisfactory. The most of the theology of the Church, so far as its Christological aspect has been concerned, has been the attempt to relate the Jesus of history to the idea of God which prevailed at any given period in the history of thought. This accounts for the fact that much of this theology never has and never can square with the New Testament portrait of Jesus. The new theology is interested in the interpretation of God in terms of Jesus. Most of our theology has come out of periods of conflict and controversy and has suffered both from overemphasis and understatement. The aim of theology has been the intelligible expression of Christian truth and thought in terms of the hour. The present unsettled state of traditional theology, and the fact

22

that its answer to the question about Jesus is not clear enough or unanimous enough to be adequate, is the result of the "clashing of confused efforts to obtain this end in churches which are mostly organized on the basis of fixed intellectual forms."

The answer that Jesus is human and only human is not a new answer. There have always been those who believe that "Jesus is only a man, a truly wonderful man, but only a man." Emerson held this view and put Jesus on the same level with Plato, Cæsar, and Shakespeare. Dr. John Haynes Holmes, one of the ablest preachers of our day, holds this view. He classes Jesus with St. Francis of Assisi and Mahatma Gandhi as being only a man. A religious genius, to be sure, just as these other men are; but "human as we are human, a man as we are men, a figure of history like a thousand others." Modern humanism has made much of this view, and has given it a prominence which it had not enjoyed for years. There is something beautiful and compellingly attractive about this human Jesus. But all the lines and shades and colors do not appear in the picture. Dr. Walter Russell Bowie calls the Jesus who is portrayed in Professor Case's new book, "Jesus: A New Biography," an "uncertain and circumscribed figure"; and this same thing might be said of much of the modern literature about Jesus which keeps its eye only upon his humanity. One lays down many books which have been written about Jesus in recent years fascinated by what one writer calls his "complete and unreserved humanity," and yet with a feeling that the one thing that ought to

23

be said about Jesus, the one thing that must be said about Jesus, has been left unsaid. It is true that the men who have exalted the human Jesus from the very beginning have often kept the Church from going to dangerous extremes in the other direction. For centuries theirs was the only protest against the ghostly figure of the Christ of the creeds. It is also true that the men who in recent years have recovered for us the Jesus of history have made an invaluable contribution to the thought and life of the Church. But when they have gone as far as they can in their attempts to explain this Jesus in terms of mere humanity, there is a wistfulness in their conclusions which is almost tragic. Even though they will not admit his divinity, they are not surprised "that men have thought of him as divine." And because they have not gone on to a satisfactory conclusion concerning that "something more about Jesus" which has kept him in a class by himself for nineteen hundred years, their answer does not satisfy.

The answer that we do not know whether there was an historical Jesus, and that it does not make much difference, is no answer at all. In seeking to answer one question it raises a dozen others which cannot be answered. It is not a new answer. It emerged in the eighteenth century as a purely philosophical question. It became popular when historical criticism and the scientific method began to question the historical foundations of Christianity. Thus, when Christian doctrine came to be considered as "both philosophically unsound and historically doubtful," a new apologetic

24

emerged, the aim of which was to find a "justification for the Christian belief which would be independent of historical criticism on the one hand, and of metaphysic on the other." In this new apologetic Christianity became quite easily divorced from historic fact. From this position it was only a step to the other position that Jesus never lived at all, that the Gospels are founded upon a myth, and that those teachings which are supposed to have been the wisdom and insight of Jesus are nothing more than the "spiritual ideals of many humble and unknown men." Many have taken this step to-day, and are trying to live by and preach a so-called Christian message which is independent of all the facts of Christian history. Such a message may do for the philosophers. But careful observation leads one to conclude that the average man is neither willing nor able to divorce his religion from what he considers to be historic fact. "If his religion is to supply him with sanctions for conduct and to be judged accordingly, he can hardly be blamed if he seeks for it some basis in reality and some foundation stronger than a myth." The practical effects of the answer that Jesus never lived is to "nullify the religion in the name of which it speaks. The great need for religion in the present hour is for more and not less historic reality. Nothing is gained by telling us that we have the spirit of Jesus if we lose the historical Jesus. To the plain man this means that you have reduced his religion to the 'baseless fabric of a dream.'" The average run of people have very little use for a myth, or legend, or illusion, even if they are

25

presented as aids to religion. If men become convinced that the Church has no historic basis for the Jesus whom it presents to the world, that he has no reality or value except as "a working hypothesis of God's character," then the Church as an aggressive spiritual force will cease to be. The world will never be satisfied with a purely negative answer to the question about Jesus.

Can we find an adequate answer to the question about Jesus? I think we can, and it will not be a new answer. It is the answer of the New Testament. Christianity is an historical religion, and it must stand or fall upon its historical basis. The center of Christianity is an historical person, Jesus of Nazareth. All we know about his life and religion is found in the New Testament. In this little book, the smallest of all great books of religion, we have the record of a set of facts about Jesus and the experience out of which the record and the interpretation of these facts grew. If the critics object that the New Testament is the product of the early Church, we answer by asking them who or what created this Church. Where did that body of facts and community of experience which brought the Church to birth come from? If they object that while the New Testament may be history, it is history written with a definite purpose, we ask them how much history is not written with a definite purpose. The critics are right when they say that the New Testament gives us a Christianized conception of Jesus; they are absolutely wrong when they assume that this fact invalidates it as an historical document. The

26

New Testament is absolutely honest both in its purpose and its claims, and it is all we have. If in it we cannot find an answer to the question about Jesus, then that question must remain forever unanswered.

The Christian Church was born out of the white-hot experience of men who had known Jesus of Nazareth both before and after his death. The New Testament represents the attempt of these men and their immediate followers to put into permanent form some of the words, acts, and impressions which the facts of his life made upon them. What we have in the New Testament is a record of the facts of history worked through the crucible of a deep experience of those facts. The New Testament is not clear at all points simply because the facts which it seeks to record and interpret were so tremendous that they were for that day, and have remained for all time, inexpressible in human language. However, we may believe that the expression of these facts which we do have is sufficient.

For the authors of the first three Gospels Jesus is both the Son of Man and the Son of God. In many ways, their picture of Jesus is the most satisfactory. They present him in a perfectly natural way as a human being. All the marks of our common humanity are upon him. He is not a stranger to hunger, thirst, pity, weariness, anger, grief, and anguish of soul. The play of little children interested him, and he must have laughed often at the feasts which he attended. He was the best friend the publicans and sinners ever had, and his disciples found in him a real companion. And

27

yet, when these same writers come to present him as more than man, as so strangely perfect in his humanity that they could not fit him into human language and account for him in terms of human nature which they knew, their story is still natural. There is nothing in the Gospels which would lead the average reader to conclude that the writers are recording history when they describe the perfectly human Jesus, and using their inventive genius as literary artists when they describe the Jesus whom they came to believe was more than human. Both sides of Jesus' nature blend perfectly in the synoptic story. When these Gospels present Jesus as mingling with sinners and yet as being himself sinless, we are not surprised. When they picture him as being tempted in all points as common people are tempted, we do not think it strange that he resisted all these temptations. Even the miraculous element is a perfectly natural part of the story. Unless we come to the reading of Matthew, Mark, and Luke with a decided bias against the miraculous or supernatural aspects of the universe in which we live, the miracles do not appear to be inventions. The Jesus of these Gospels impresses us as being a personality who was so much at home in the universe of God that what his contemporaries called miracles, and what we with all our scientific knowledge of the universe must still call miracles, may not have been contrary to the fundamental laws of the universe, but only to those laws which we have not yet discovered. When we get the total picture of Jesus in the Synoptics, even the resurrection does not appear to be an invention.

28

Every one of the disciples had to be convinced, with evidence that would certainly convince even our scientific age, that the tomb in Joseph's garden was empty and that the Jesus whom they had known to be dead was actually alive again with a strange new life which they were utterly unable to account for on any other basis than that he was the Son of God.\\

For the author of Acts, Jesus was both human and divine. As a careful historian the writer of this earliest bit of Church history was recording the things which he was convinced were those most surely believed and preached by that church. The fact that he may be giving us only a free composition of Peter's Pentecost sermon and of the other preaching of the time, does not detract from their value as evidence of what the disciples believed about Jesus immediately after his death and resurrection. The Jesus of Acts is a "man approved of God" while he was on earth. This man was crucified and slain "by the hands of lawless men." He was raised up from the dead by the power of God because he could not be holden of death. This same Jesus has been exalted by God as both "Christ and Lord." The human Jesus, the crucified Jesus, the irresistible, death-conquering Christ, the exalted Lord—all that these terms imply formed the heart of the earliest Christian message about Jesus as the author of Acts found it.//

For the author of the fourth Gospel, a portrait of Jesus which was drawn toward the close of the first century, when the influence of the "strange and artificial atmosphere of the Alexandrian philosophy" was

29

beginning to influence Christian thought, and when "opinion about Jesus was beginning to crystallize," Jesus was still the human friend and companion of men. It is in this Gospel that Jesus calls his disciples friends and that that intimate relationship between them is emphasized. If we had no other Gospel than this, we would still have a matchless picture of the perfectly human Jesus. But in this Gospel it is the divine side of Jesus' life and nature that receives the chief emphasis. In fact, the writer of this Gospel makes it perfectly clear that he is not writing a life of Jesus, but laying the foundation for a theology of Jesus. He admits that there are many words of Jesus, and many incidents in his life, which are not included in his Gospel. What he has selected and written "are written that ye may believe that Jesus is the Christ, the Son of God." For this writer Jesus is "the way, the truth, and the life." He would have men see God in Jesus Christ, and through Jesus men were to have their only entry into the presence of the Father.

For Paul, Jesus was first of all "the man of Galilee," who was "born of the seed of David according to the flesh." It is probably true that Paul's first contact was with the "risen Christ," for we cannot be sure that he ever knew the human Jesus. But this need not lead us to the conclusion, which some have reached, that because Paul first knew the risen Christ, he therefore had no interest in the history of Jesus. Paul's argument for the resurrection of Jesus, the earliest and perhaps the greatest Christian argument for the resurrection, rests not upon his theory of the

risen Christ, but upon the basis of the facts about
the resurrection which he had gleaned after careful
investigation among those who had been eyewitnesses
to the life of Jesus both before and after the resurrection. When Paul writes about the relation of Jesus
to the Father in some of his letters, he writes as a
theologian. When he writes about the resurrection of
Jesus from the dead, he writes as an historian whose
conclusions are based upon facts. For Paul, Jesus
was also the Son of God. He was transformed from
Saul the Hebrew to Paul the Christian through the
revelation of God, the reflection of God which he saw
"in the face of Jesus Christ." In Paul's thought, God
was "the Father of our Lord Jesus Christ." And this
Jesus who was the Son of God became the supreme
Lord and Master of the soul of Paul. While much of
the Christology of Paul is stated in theological language, it was more than mere theology. It was the
attempt of one of the most brilliant intellects of the
first century to account for a body of historical facts
which he had investigated for himself, and for an experience of a living personality who had completely
changed his own personality.

The answer which we have suggested to the question about Jesus is not a new answer. But a survey
of the history of the Church and of Christian thought
during the last nineteen hundred years leads us to believe that it is the only adequate answer. The new
answers to the question about Jesus have never been
fruitful in the life of the Church. Where men have
followed them to their logical conclusions one of two

31

things has happened: either these men have left the Church altogether, or the churches which they have tried to lead have been powerless so far as any effective Christian witness was concerned. The great seasons of revival and power in the history of Christianity have come as the result of a return to this old answer. In the beginning it was a stumblingblock to the Jews and foolishness to the Gentiles; to-day it will appear to be a stumblingblock to rationalism and scientific dogmatism, and plain foolishness to the leaders of a civilization of material wealth and success. But it was in the beginning, has been for all Christian history, and will be for the centuries to come, "the power of God unto salvation," both individual and social, for all those who will receive it.

A few years ago Joyce Kilmer gave the world this fine thought in verse:

"The scene shall never fit the deed,
    Grotesquely, wonders come to pass.
The fool shall mount an Arab steed,
    And Jesus ride upon an ass."

A religious editor has this fine comment upon these lines: "It is a worthy reminder, for in this world of noise and bustle and big business the spectacular too often catches the popular fancy and leads men to forget the quiet and often unseen forces which slowly but surely are affecting the world for good. The figure of Christ upon an ass is by no means that of a mighty conqueror. An Arab steed gayly caparisoned would have been far more fitting for one who in a few short

32

days was to say to his companions, 'Fear not, for I have overcome the world.' On that ass he did not bear any resemblance to a conqueror even though the populace greeted him with hosannas. Yet no entry ever made into any city was more portentous than that entry of Christ into Jerusalem on the back of an ass. The clatter of the hoofs of the Arab steeds on which the mighty conquerors of the world have ridden has died away into silence. But the patter of the footsteps of a common ass has resounded throughout the world for nineteen hundred years and will resound throughout all time.''

So it will be with this old answer to the question of Jesus. For some, perhaps for many in our sophisticated age, it may seem grotesque and even foolish to suggest it. But we have suggested it in the firm conviction that when all these other answers have died away in the silence of the years, the New Testament answer will still be fresh, powerful, and sufficient.

BY WHAT AUTHORITY?

"And when he was come into the temple, the chief priests and the elders of the people came unto him as he was teaching, and said, By what authority doest thou these things? and who gave thee this authority?"

MATTHEW 21: 23.

II

BY WHAT AUTHORITY?

THIS WAS a perfectly natural question for these leaders of orthodox and institutionalized religion to ask. These men recognized in Jesus a teacher of unusual ability. His influence with the people bothered them. They did not deny the fact that he had authority. They simply wanted to know the source of this authority. The multitudes had listened to Jesus and marveled because "he taught them as one having authority, and not as the scribes." These same men who asked this question had sent officers to arrest Jesus, and those officers had come back empty-handed, giving as their excuse for not having taken him only this, "Never man spake like this man." These religious leaders who were puzzled by this strange new authority of Jesus thought that all religious authority had been intrusted to them and resided in their religious institutions. They, and the people, understood the teachings of the scribes. These scribes were men whose business it was to master the law. "They packed their mental lockers with statutes, and rules, and precepts; with thousands of jots and tittles. They were just incarnate codes of law. When they gave counsel to anybody it was always just a bit of legality, always a fragment of tradition, something taken down from the dusty shelves of the past."

Jesus was not like that. There was something about what he offered the people that had a strange influence over them. There was something so new, and original, and immediate about his teaching that men instinctively felt the authority of both the words and the teacher. As E. Stanley Jones puts it in his book, *The Christ of the Mount,* "The scribes taught rules of religion; Jesus taught 'them.' . . . The scribes quoted authorities. Jesus spake out of the authority of living reality. In the words of the scribes they heard the voice of the past; in the words of Jesus they heard the Voice that assumed control over the past, the present, and the future." When Jesus spoke he was "trafficking with the primitive secrets of life," and always there was something in his words which, to his hearers, "seemed to run parallel to the controlling law and order of the universe." Jesus always unveiled for his hearers what seemed to be "little strata of the fundamental constitution of the world." His authority was self-evident. It is quite probable that up to this time the teachings of Jesus had only come to the chief priests and elders secondhand. And perhaps they had wondered why the multitudes and the officers had been so completely carried away with his words. Now they had listened for themselves and had known the strange power and authority of

38

those words. And they wanted to know what was back of them and by what right they were uttered.

Jesus answered this question about authority by asking another question. He asked his questioners to tell him whether the baptism of John was "from heaven, or of men." "And they reasoned with themselves, saying, if we shall say, From heaven; he will say unto us, Why then did ye not believe him? But if we shall say, From men; we fear the people; for all hold John as a prophet. And they answered Jesus, and said, We cannot tell. And he said unto them, Neither tell I you by what authority I do these things." Perhaps we will never know just why Jesus refused to give a definite answer to this question. We do know that when men approached Jesus in the spirit of controversy they never got much satisfaction out of him. In the presence of Jesus the "openly hostile" and the "merely curious and trifling" were only made to feel how utterly insincere they really were. Some reasons for Jesus' refusal have been suggested. Perhaps he refused because he saw clearly that these men were incapable of understanding him. There was such a wide gulf between the authority of which they boasted and the authority by which he lived and taught that they could never bridge it. And then, again, it may have been the evident insincerity of these men which called forth Jesus' refusal. Jesus knew these men were trying to trap him. They were looking for a pretext for getting him out of their way. If he had said, "My authority is that of the Son of God," they would have said, as they did say later, that such a claim was preposterous and blasphemous. He refused to allow them to escape by "merely raising a dust about a matter on the abstract or intellectual plane." A few have advanced the theory that Jesus did not answer this question because he was not conscious of having any special authority either for his life or his message. But whatever the reason for Jesus' refusal, the men who asked the question were not satisfied. When he had finished a group of searching parables pointed directly at them, had it not been for their fear of the people, they would have laid hold of him then and there and put him out of their way by force.

The question about authority is one of the most fundamental questions in the life of the race. It goes to the very roots of history, government, philosophy, science, and religion. We are interested in the question now only as it has to do with religion, and with that religion which is called Christianity. In the clash between the Jewish leaders and Jesus we have an example of that eternal conflict between a religion of authority and a religion of free and unfettered souls. These men looked upon themselves as the custodians of the only religious authority which was valid—the authority of the faith and the traditions of their fathers. In Jesus we have an individual who refused to follow the multitude in a willing acceptance of that faith and tradition—an individual who insisted upon stepping outside the established bounds and going beyond the commonplace mass in his dreaming and thinking. Naturally he was looked upon as a dangerous character. A genuine appreciation and understanding of Jesus will always be dangerous for that type of religious authority which challenged him in Jerusalem.

The question about the source of authority in Christianity is a very real one to-day. The clash now is not between the representatives of the Jews and Jesus, for the priesthood and the institution in which that authority rested has long since perished from the earth. The present clash is between Jesus and those representatives of his own Church who have sought to make his religion one of authority rather than of the spirit. It is a clash between those who have embalmed Jesus in an authoritative institution or system of thought, and those unfettered spirits who are seeking to interpret the life and teachings of Jesus free from the hand of tradition and dogmatic authority. In our day the pressure of external authority in the Christian religion is definitely on the wane. In the modern desire and quest for new truth in every field, there is an aggressive reaction against all shams and half-truths no matter how firmly they may be intrenched behind authority. As someone has put it, "There is a feeling that when we tear away the conventions and prejudices, who knows what amazing truths may be revealed?" There have been periods in the history of Christianity when, like the doctrine of the divine right of kings, the idea of the divine right of religious institutions and creeds was unquestioned by all but a very few. The theory of the divine right of kings is dead, and the theory of the divine right of religious institutions to sit in judgment upon what

41

men shall or shall not believe is destined to meet the same fate. For multitudes of people, both in and out of the Church, who look with favor upon the religion of Jesus as the only hope of the race, the old external authority is gone forever. And who, even in his most conservative mood, would want to restore this authority even if he could? The dead should be left to bury their dead. But we face utter failure and chaos unless we can find a real basis for a religious authority, or sanction if you want to call it that, which will take the place of the one which is gone.

In the long history of Christianity men have appealed to different sources of authority. In the beginning it was Jesus himself. He was the foundation and head of the Church. He was the source of its abounding zeal and conquering power. The earliest name which was attached to the believers as a group was "the Church of Christ." The authority of the early Christians was the authority of a Person whom men considered to be both Son of Man and Son of God. The men who became the first leaders in the Church were the same men who had listened to Jesus teach and who had left all to follow him because "he taught as one having authority." Whether Jesus uttered the words, "All authority hath been given unto me. . . . Go ye . . ." or whether they simply express what the writers of the Gospels believed about Jesus, the result is the same. No matter who was responsible for those words, they give us an accurate picture of the source of authority in the primitive Church. For those original apostles and their immediate followers,

42

many of whom gave their lives for the sake of the gospel, Jesus did possess all authority. It was in the name of Jesus that they rebuked and called to repentance the very men who had crucified him, and it was in his name they offered salvation to the whole world. They worshiped on the first day of the week in honor of his resurrection; they used the ancient practice of immersion in water as the symbol of the new life in Christ because it so perfectly typified the death, burial, and resurrection; and they met around the table to break the bread and drink from the cup in memory of him. The only authority the first Christian community knew anything about was the authority of its risen Lord. The leaders of the early Church did not look upon the authority of Jesus as something which he had left with them to incase in doctrines and creeds and impose upon future generations, but as something to which they themselves might look for power to preach the gospel to the ends of the earth. It was an authority to be acted upon and not to be forced upon others.

Very soon, however, under the influence of Greek philosophy and the common weaknesses of human nature, the source of authority in Christianity shifted from a living Person to a set of intellectual statements about that Person. For a time the authority of the historic creeds was supreme. The next shift finds the source of authority in an infallible Church. The authority of the creeds was still valid, but the Church now had the power to interpret these creeds as it saw fit, and its word was final. For centuries there was

43

no appeal from this source of authority, and it was exercised and enforced in a ruthless manner. The Church took on all the marks of an imperial organization. Even kings and emperors bowed before its popes in both spiritual and temporal matters. For centuries the infallible pope of this infallible Church was the most powerful man on earth. His word was the word of both God and man. This authority was, perhaps, as nearly supreme over the lives and minds of men as any external authority has ever been. When the authority of an infallible Church was challenged, and for a part of Christendom was finally broken, there emerged to take its place the authority of an inerrant Bible. The scriptures of both the Old and the New Testaments had been looked upon as inspired documents before. But now for the first time the claim for absolute inerrancy was made for them. This appeal to the Bible as a verbally inspired book, and as the chief source of authority in Christianity was an appeal of necessity. The leaders of the Protestant Reformation and their immediate followers were up against an infallible Church. They had to find some unquestionable source of authority which they could match against that infallibility. However, this theory of authority soon led to some of the very same abuses which it sought to correct. Men were persecuted and even burned to the stake in the name of an inerrant Book. As a protest against both an infallible Church and a verbally inspired Bible, the source of authority shifted to the enlightened human reason. This shift brings us down to the beginning of the modern period.

44

The enlightened human reason is still considered by many to be the final source of authority in religion. But where this reason has depended upon the deductive method of the older systems of philosophy it is rapidly being replaced to-day by the scientific method and the laboratory. For many, in our day, the laboratory has the final word in religion as well as in other things. Both the Church and the Bible are being subjected to very severe criticism at the hands of a human reason which has adopted the method and the findings of the laboratory. And any theory of authority which expects to stand in our modern world cannot entirely ignore the claims of this human reason.

Our age demands a religion and a religious authority which have their roots in history. The modern mind will not accept any religious authority which cannot stand the light of historical research and the scientific method. Every claim of religion for the mastery over the minds of men or for the guidance of their lives, if it is to have the weight of authority, must be grounded in historic reality. Because this is true, we believe the only basis of authority in Christianity which will meet the modern demand is Jesus himself—the authority of a person who actually lived on this earth and who has established himself as an unquestionable part of history. We are convinced that we must shift clear back to the original source of authority in Christianity as being the surest if not the only hope for the future. We know more about persons than anything else. The only contacts that really matter in our lives are the contacts with other person-

45

alities. Aside from personality there is no history. The history of the physical universe and even of life itself would be meaningless if it were not for personality. "The world moves by personality. All the great currents of history have flowed from persons. Organization is powerful; but no organization has ever accomplished anything until a person has stood at the center of it and filled it with his thought, with his life. Truth is mighty and must prevail. But it never does prevail actually until it gets itself embodied, incarnated in a personality."

The authority of the early Church was a factual authority. It was not the authority of a doctrine which was believed, but the authority of a Person who lived, died, and was alive again. "A non-existent Christianity did not spring out of the air and create a Christ. A real Christ appeared in the world and created Christianity." In spite of all the critics Jesus stands firmly in the thought and life of the race as an historical person.

> "The Word had breath, and wrought
> With human hands the Creed of Creeds,
> In loveliness of perfect deeds,
> More strong than all poetic thought."

What was and is this authority of Jesus to which we must appeal? It is the authority of a Person who lived as no other person has ever lived. It is the authority of a Person who "spake as never man spake." It is the authority of a Person who was superior to death

46

and who lives forever in vital contact with the life of the race.

The words of Pilate, "Behold the Man," spoken before an angry mob "in one of the most dramatic moments in human history," have become the classic expression of the world's estimate of the Man Jesus Christ. Other religions have produced great personalities, but you will not find his superior or his equal among them. History is replete with the names of men who have held the center of the world's stage for a season and whose commanding personality and genius have given them extraordinary power and influence over their fellows. But that power and influence has always been sectional and local rather than universal. The thought and the literature of the centuries, both sacred and secular (if we are ever justified in making any such distinction), combine to pay tribute to the life of Jesus as the most commanding life that was ever lived upon this earth.

One of the finest of the recent tributes to the life of Jesus comes from Dr. Friedrich Rittelmeyer, in his splendid book, *Behold the Man*. His portrait of the Life, the Personality, the Message, and the Significance of Jesus is one that has challenged much of our recent superficial thinking about Jesus. According to Dr. Rittelmeyer the life of Jesus was a life "unanalyzable in kind and unfathomable in richness, but capable of becoming visibly intertwined with the material of external events and of weaving itself ineradicably into the texture of our world's history." "Do we claim too much," he asks, "when we say that Jesus was the

47

first man of us to feel what living really means, what
human life is meant to be, could be, and at its core
really wants to be? . . . The life of Jesus makes us
feel that there is a point in cosmic history where human
life tends to exceed its previous bounds and becomes
exalted to a higher plane of vision and understanding.''
Has our modern world gone beyond this life of lives?
Dr. Rittelmeyer thinks not.   Our ideas have changed.
Our points of emphasis in thought have changed.   The
limits of the human mind have become evident and the
spiritual faculties have developed a greater degree of
susceptibility.   Nature has become more familiar to
us, and the universe infinitely larger.   ''What has been
the effect of these immense changes toward our attitude
toward Jesus?   We reply that, in spite of these extraordinary revolutions in our intellectual world, Jesus
still captivates the human race with the splendor of
the divine which radiates from him.   His image has
become brighter and more vivid, that is all.   Still he
waits with a welcome all his own for those who seek
God, waits for those who seek true humanity.   A dis-
covery without parallel is in store for him who, in
some hour of calm, penetrates all the theories of the
centuries and comes out face to face with the human
glory of Jesus.   This man once did live here!   This
man once did walk our earth!   There is a thought with
substance enough to grip us our whole life long.''

The authority of Jesus is the authority of a Person
who ''spake as never man spake.''   No other religion
has presented the world with a message comparable
with the teachings of Jesus.   When we compare Jesus

48

as a teacher with the other great teachers of the race, we discover that he is in a class by himself. The material of his message, the body of his teaching, was not culled from the various branches of human knowledge common in his day. He did not quote from books, except the Old Testament. Every word which he uttered bears the stamp of immediate contact with reality. As someone has put it, "He was not a commentator on truths already revealed. He was a revealer of new truth. His teaching was not the exposition; it was the text. . . . What he said was meant to be its own evidence. His teaching is neither ancient nor modern, neither deductive nor inductive, neither Jewish nor Greek. It is universal, enduring, valid for all minds and all times." In Jesus the teacher we have the strange and unequaled phenomenon of a man who, "without writing a single line, set more pens in motion, and furnished themes for more sermons, orations, discussions, learned volumes, works of art, and songs of praise than the whole army of great men of ancient and modern times."

The intellects of the centuries have never been able to exhaust the meaning of the words of Jesus. Appealing again to Dr. Rittelmeyer's estimate of Jesus, we find him saying: "Never do intellect, feeling, and will exhaust the content of his words. Ever rings out clear an intonation of his soul, intelligible to the most simple-minded, and yet too profound for those most richly endowed, far beyond all and yet wholly strange to none. . . . Even when Jesus seems to be absorbed in the description of our ordinary human

49

world, one always feels the high world of God at its back. While we think we are simply listening to an everyday story the sunshine of a higher world is creeping into our souls. . . . Jesus was no formal teacher, but the beacon to new altitudes of reality.'' In his recent study of the Sermon on the Mount, E. Stanley Jones quotes Rodin, the great sculptor, as saying, ''Beyond Phidias art does not progress,'' and goes on to say: ''Beyond Christ religion or moral progress does not go. . . . If this Sermon on the Mount is his mind, then this is a mount for humanity to scale in the future and not a foothill which humanity has explored and transcended. . . . The only objection that we can bring against Christ is that his life is too lofty, and too grand, and his mind too demanding of us. Our very objection proves that he is ahead of us and not behind us.''

The authority of Jesus is the authority of a Person who was superior to death and who is alive forevermore. This Jesus who inspired the seer of Patmos to write words of encouragement to his persecuted brethren by his declaration, ''I am the first and the last, the living one: and I was dead, and behold I am alive forevermore,'' is still the greatest inspiration of his Church. The authority of his matchless life and his unique and unusual message greatly impressed his immediate followers. But it was the authority of his risen life that inspired them to leave us the record of his earthly career and message. The authority of the human Jesus, fascinating as it is; and the

50

authority of his message, powerful as it is—these have never been quite sufficient and are not sufficient for our day.

In one of the chapters in his *Productive Beliefs,* Dr. Lynn Harold Hough characterizes Jesus as "The Imperial Personality." When you stand in the presence of Jesus, he points out, "you have a strange feeling that he had no right to die. At least you have a feeling that he cannot stay dead. The life he lived propels itself forward. The whole impact of his personality is so vital, so magnetic, so supremely powerful in all ethical and spiritual things, the unutterable dynamic which went out from him: all these seem incompatible with death. You are not surprised when you hear the resurrection story. . . . The broken tomb seems natural for him. It would seem unbelievable in any one else." But, he goes on to say, "at the same time one must admit that belief in the resurrection must meet one great test. That is not the analysis of the resurrection stories, though that analysis is legitimate enough. The real test is this: Has anything gone forth into the life of the world from this personality so unique and high and transforming that this tremendous influence in some genuine fashion validates the belief in the resurrection?" Dr. Hough answers this question in the affirmative, and it is just this fact, that the belief in the risen, living Christ has been such a productive force in the life of the world for nineteen hundred years, that makes the resurrection of Jesus one of the unmistakable marks of his authority. This man who was superior to death, who in his inmost soul was so "at one with God" that he "could not be holden of death," has exercised and continues to exercise a strange authority over the souls of men which cannot be explained in our purely human categories.

Such is the authority of Jesus Christ. Says Dr. John A. Hutton: "Wherever he has come to be really known, he has come to be acknowledged as the supreme authority for man in things pertaining to God. In human societies where Jesus has really entered as a force and spirit, men may continue to order their lives in ways which he does not approve; but if such men have really become aware of Christ, they are not able—except by doing violence to certain delicate but fundamental susceptibilities—to rid themselves of a haunting accusation and moral uneasiness. . . . They may sit down to life as to a feast; but nothing has its true taste and relish for them so long as they know that there is one, Jesus Christ, whom they cannot honestly ask to sit down with them. And because of the averted face of that Son of Man, they know that they are not at home, that they are not living naturally and candidly, that they are avoiding an entire world of reality within which and through which, as they suspect, a man comes to God if he can come unto God at all."

Many will still insist upon the authority of an infallible Church, an inerrant Bible, the enlightened human reason, or the laboratory as their chief source of authority in religion. We would not disturb them. But for those who no longer find one or all of these a

sufficient basis for their faith, and who are looking
for a more valid source of authority, we offer that
which was sufficient for the first Christians. In this
Person, Jesus Christ, in whose praise men have ex-
hausted the language of the centuries, we have our
highest and most adequate source of religious authority. His absolute confidence in the trustworthiness of
God and his faith in the dependability of the universe
have never been equaled; his love for humanity and the
manifestation of that love in unselfish service and
heroic sacrifice have never been surpassed; his stain-
less character has never been matched; no words which
have ever fallen from human lips are to be compared
with his words; and the power of his endless life cannot be evaded or avoided. In an hour when all the
odds were against him he said calmly to his troubled
followers, ''Be of good cheer; I have overcome the
world.'' And in an hour of sublime faith he said, ''And
I, if I be lifted up from the earth, will draw all men
unto myself.''

When the Church discovers for itself this confidence and faith of Jesus; when it is willing to have its
whole life dominated by his love and to lose itself in
unselfish service and heroic sacrifice for the world;
when the character of its members begins to approach
the stainlessness of his character; and when the power
of his endless life becomes its possession—then it will
have found a valid authority for its life and work.
And when in an hour of heroic adventure it asserts its
mastery over the forces of this world, and in an hour
of sublime faith exalts Jesus Christ high above all

53

that is purely earthly in its organization and doctrine, so the world can really see him and know him for what he was to the first Christians and what he is for all time, it will have given to the world its final source of religious authority.

GOD OR CÆSAR?

*"Tell us therefore, What
thinkest thou? Is it lawful
to give tribute unto Cæsar,
or not?"*

MATTHEW 22: 17.

III

GOD OR CÆSAR?

FOLLOWING THEIR UTTER DEFEAT over the question about authority, the enemies of Jesus came back later in the day with a series of three "crafty questions," hoping thus to entrap him and discredit him in the eyes of the multitudes. The first of these questions had to do with the payment of tribute to Cæsar. Some of the Jewish leaders held that it was wrong to pay taxes to a pagan government. Another group, the Herodians, who owed their power to the empire, thought it was right. Both of these groups were represented among those who questioned Jesus. They approached him with flattering words. "Teacher, we know that thou art true, and teachest the way of God in true and carest not for any one: for thou regardest not the person of men." The majority of the people sided with those leaders who hated the oppressive taxation of Rome, and, these questioners reasoned, if he answers this question in the affirmative, he will bring down upon himself the displeasure of the people. But, if he answers in the negative, the Herodians will have a clear case against him and be able to report him to the Roman governor as a man who is against the empire. They figured that they had a perfect case. The trap was so skillfully set that they would catch their victim either coming or going.

But again, Jesus proved himself too much for them. Again, he beat them at their own game. Taking a Roman coin from them, he said, "Whose is this image and superscription?" They answered, "Cæsar's." "Then said he unto them, Render therefore unto Cæsar the things that are Cæsar's; and unto God the things that are God's." They were using Cæsar's coins. They were accepting the protection of Cæsar's armies and laws. They were enjoying all the advantages of Roman civilization in one of the most peaceful periods in the history of the ancient world. They owed something for that. They were under obligation to pay taxes for that.

But Jesus did not stop there. For him, there was One who was greater than Cæsar—God. As human souls these men had stamped upon them the image of this God. They were his creatures, his children. Without this God, the civilization of which the Romans boasted could not have existed. These men were concerned about coins of silver and gold which are perishable. Jesus was concerned about the imperishable souls of men. When all the silver and gold and power of Rome would be forgotten, Jesus knew that the souls of men would still be the most valuable and eternal things in the universe. To the Creator and Sustainer of these souls, God, men owe something. Jesus went deeper than the mere question of taxes or tribute.

He went deeper than the question of man's common duties and obligations as a citizen of the state. He took all these for granted. He went down where the deepest loyalties of life lie, where men must decide where their first allegiance really is. He raised the question as to whether God or the State, conscience or nationalism, comes first. And he left the distinct impression, an impression which has been the basis of all the real religious liberty the world has ever known and enjoyed, that there is a realm in the human soul where the state has no right to intrude and press its demands for absolute allegiance. "And when they heard it, they marveled, and left him, and went away."

What Jesus said here was in keeping with the tone and tenor of his whole message. For Jesus, God came first. His gospel was a "gospel of God." In the presence of God and others who would be masters, Jesus said, "No servant can serve two masters; for either he will hate the one, and love the other; or else he will hold to the one, and despise the other. Ye cannot serve God and mammon." When men came to him and offered to become his disciples with clear-cut reservations in the offer, he said, "No man, having put his hand to the plow, and looking back, is fit for the kingdom of God." To those who had any reservations whatsoever in their minds, Jesus said, "If any man cometh unto me, and hateth not his own father, and mother, and wife, and children, and brethren, and sisters, yea, and his own life also, he cannot be my disciple." Professor Bundy is probably right in holding that such uncompromising demands as these,

59

demands which strike the modern mind as "impossible, even fanatical," are "primarily autobiographical in substance, they amount to personal confessions." But this does not soften or make them any the less exacting. Jesus had completely dedicated his life to the Father, and all his powers had been consecrated to the kingdom of God, and "both for himself and others he was absolutely uncompromising when the issues of the kingdom of God were at stake. . . . He tolerates no excuses; he allows no exceptions; there are no if's and and's. He sets his followers, as he has set himself, before an unconditional either . . . or."

The early Christians caught this spirit of Jesus and built it firmly into the life of the Church. You will not find any spirit of compromise in the preaching which is recorded in Acts. Back of all that Peter said at Pentecost was an absolute loyalty to the God of Jesus. He preached that day, not in the name of men, but in the name of God. And it was the feeling that it was God's message, rather than Peter's, which brought conviction to the hearts of his hearers and secured such marvelous results. When Peter and John were arrested and brought before the authorities for the first time and were charged not to speak or teach again in the name of Jesus, they answered, "Whether it is right in the sight of God to hearken unto you rather than God, judge ye: for we cannot but speak the things which we have seen and heard." When they came before these leaders again, "the high priest asked them, saying, We strictly charged you not to teach in this name: and behold, ye have filled Jerusalem with your teaching, and intend to bring this man's blood upon us. But Peter and the apostles answered and said, We must obey God rather than men." And "when they beat them, and charged them not to speak in the name of Jesus, . . . they therefore departed from the presence of the council, rejoicing that they were counted worthy to suffer dishonor for the Name. And every day, in the temple and at home, they ceased not to teach and to preach Jesus as the Christ."

It was this absolute allegiance to God which brought on the fierce conflict between Christianity and the Roman Empire. At first, Christianity was tolerated by the empire. While Jesus was alive the Roman governor paid very little attention to him. The Jews clinched their argument before Pilate by representing Jesus, not as a religious teacher, but as a disturber in the empire, as a contender for the throne of Cæsar. "If you let this man go," they said, "you are not Cæsar's friend." Following the resurrection the Jews opposed the Christians bitterly on purely religious grounds. There is little evidence that the Roman authorities were interested in this religious clash between the Jews and the Christians. It was only when the Christians were represented as teaching or practicing that which was opposed to or which would endanger the power of Cæsar that the Roman officials acted. In Philippi, Paul and Silas were brought before the rulers on this charge: "These men do exceedingly trouble our city, and set forth customs which it is not lawful for us to receive, or to observe, being Romans." And in Thessalonica the Jews were able to throw the whole city into an uproar by accusing Paul and Silas of being enemies of Cæsar. They brought Jason, who had received Paul and Silas into his home, before the rulers and said, "These that have turned the world upside down are come hither also. . . . And they all act contrary to the decrees of Cæsar, saying that there is another king, one Jesus."

Rome tolerated all religions. But when Rome, with her worship of Cæsar as God, began to realize that here was a religion which could not be bent to the Roman mind, and whose followers would not worship Cæsar, she began to take notice. And this notice was followed by action. Then began the long and bloody conflict between the nationalism of Rome with Cæsar as its god and the religion of Jesus which refused to recognize any god except "the God and Father of Jesus Christ." It was God or Cæsar. And the Church chose to worship God rather than Cæsar. This was a religion which Rome could not tolerate, for it undermined the very foundations upon which the imperialistic state rested. There are no records which lead us to believe that the early Christians in general refused to pay tribute to Cæsar and to assume all of the ordinary obligations of citizenship in the empire. Except in a few cases they were not accused of being revolutionists and trouble-makers. The vast majority of the members of the early Church were undoubtedly industrious and law-abiding citizens. And those who had not attained unto citizenship were not classed among the lawless. We doubt if much of a case can be made out for the contention that from the beginning

62

all Christians refused to do military service. There were many Christians in the Roman armies, and by the end of the second century some Christians were holding high official position in the empire. It was the absolute refusal of the Christians to offer sacrifices to Cæsar as god that caused Rome to act so drastically in its attempt to stamp out the Christian community. And because these Christians refused to compromise at this point, when the dust of the conflict had cleared away, God had taken the place of Cæsar rather than Cæsar taking the place of God.

This conflict between Christianity and nationalism has continued down through the centuries. The Church has not always been, "as Christianity's most characteristic creation," either "the rival of the state, or else its uncongenial associate in earthly affairs. In the Medieval Church they were combined." The Reformation which came to its head in the protests of Luther was a contest between the rights of the Christian conscience and the state. When Luther faced his enemies at Worms and said, "Here I stand; I can do no other; God help me, amen!" he was talking to an emperor and an imperial diet, the highest civil authorities of his time. One of the greatest tragedies of history is the fact that the leaders who followed Luther, and who were responsible for the great Protestant religious bodies, almost every one of them, later entered into alliances with the state which caused them to surrender their freedom of conscience. In this respect Luther himself was the most guilty of all. It is with a deep sense of disappointment that the student of history has to admit that the Reformation, which broke the power of Rome and did so much to increase the liberty of the individual, really set the clock back rather than forward so far as the conflict between Christianity and nationalism was concerned. The Reformation was far more than a theological and ecclesiastical movement. Out of the Reformation came the enormous growth of nationalism which has culminated in our day.

How about Christianity and nationalism to-day? Is this question about nationalism a vital one in the twentieth century? We believe that the issue between God and Cæsar, Christianity and nationalism, is just as clearly drawn in this century as it was in the first. The line of battle between the Church and the State is just as definitely drawn as it was in the day when the Church was fighting for its life against the power of Rome, and the results of this present conflict will be just as far-reaching in their influence upon human society as were the results of that early conflict. Such modern prophets as Dr. Harry F. Ward, Dr. Harry Emerson Fosdick, Dr. Halford E. Luccock, and many others, are agreed that we are worshiping "the nationalistic state as god," just as surely as they did in imperial Rome, and that our children's children will realize, whether we do or not, that "Christianity's most crucial fight" in the twentieth century was against the dogma of nationalism. During the World War nationalism took command of everything, including the churches, and since the war it has steadily extended "its dominion over the individual conscience,"

64

not only in civil but in religious matters as well. Dr. Fosdick reaches the conclusion that this dogma of nationalism, "as it has developed in the last two centuries, has become a complete religion," and is "the most dangerous rival of Christian principles on earth." Dr. Luccock thinks that "the shameful story of the violations of civil liberties in the United States since the Great War and respect for the rights of minority groups" is due to an aggressive nationalism which is trying to supplant Christianity and which is receiving the unquestioned veneration usually associated with religion.

Here is a modern novelist's conception of this state which has been exalted to the place of god. H. M. Tomlinson, in his story, *All Our Yesterdays,* puts these words into the mouth of an aged minister who is nearing the end of his career: "My church is down. My God has been deposed again. They've got another God now, the state, the State Almighty. I tell you that god will be worse than Moloch. You had better keep that in mind. It has no vision. It has only expediency. It has no morality, only power. And it will have no arts, for it will punish the free spirit with death. It will allow no freedom, only uniformity. Its altar will be a ballot box, and that will be a lie. Right before us is its pillar of fire. It has a heart of gunmetal and its belly is full of wheels. You will have to face the brute, you will have to face it. It is nothing but the worst of us, lifted up. The children are being bred to it."

If one is tempted to call these statements exaggerations or caricatures, he has only to read the records of the Macintosh case in our Supreme Court. When Professor Macintosh applied for citizenship he made it clear that he would not take up arms in a war which he believed was contrary to the will of God. He thought he was asking nothing more than the Constitution of the United States granted to its citizens. But the Supreme Court thought otherwise. After a lengthy discussion of the issues involved in the case, much of which seems to be decidedly far-fetched in the light of the evidence, the Court came to this conclusion: "When he [Dr. Macintosh] speaks of putting his allegiance to the will of God above the allegiance to the government, it is evident . . . that he means to make his own interpretation of the will of God the decisive test. . . . We are a nation with the duty to survive; a nation whose constitution contemplates war as well as peace; whose government must go forward upon the assumption, and safely can proceed upon no other, that unqualified allegiance to the nation and submission and obedience to the laws of the land, as well those for war as those made for peace, are not inconsistent with the will of God."

Let us not deceive ourselves about this question. It is the voice of the state exalted to the place of God. As a citizen I may worship God according to the dictates of my own conscience. I may say pretty prayers to God as often as I desire to do so. But when it comes to the matter of obeying the will of God, then I must apply to the state to find out what the will of God is. The state is absolutely infallible. No matter

66

what laws it may make either in times of war or peace, it can never be inconsistent with the will of God for the citizen to obey those laws without question. The state must go forward upon that assumption, and all of its citizens must accept that assumption as final. The state must survive regardless of God. This is a decision from which there is no appeal. The Supreme Court has spoken, and so shall it be.

What becomes of our boasted religious liberty under such a decision as this? It has simply ceased to be here in America. The burden of the dissenting opinion of the court in this case, which was written by Chief Justice Hughes, is that the principle upon which this decision rests is not inherent in the constitution. "One cannot speak of religious liberty," he says, "with proper appreciation of its essential and historic significance, without assuming a belief in supreme allegiance to the will of God." It is this priceless heritage and tradition which the Supreme Court denies and ignores in the name of nationalism. Says the *Christian Century* editorially: "It stretches over all citizens the pagan panoply of a nationalistic God before whom all must bow in reverence. . . . Prussianism never exceeded it. It is the modern equivalent of emperor worship which sent thousands of early Christians to the lions and the flames." The average American citizen who has boasted of his religious liberty has been rudely awakened. It now develops that, instead of making our religious liberty safe and sure, the constitution clothes Congress and the Supreme Court with infallible authority to interpret and declare

67

the will of God for all our citizens. It is just too bad for God so far as the United States is concerned. Fortunately, for most of us, the modern lions to which those who do not agree with this decision are thrown are nothing worse than the professional patriots, and the modern flames only the scorn of a visionless and subservient press. But the end is not yet.

What shall we do in the face of this modern rival of Christianity? Two things must be done. First of all, the individual Christian and the citizen must resist this encroachment of the nationalistic state into that realm of conscience where Jesus held it had no right to come. As Christians we must pay tribute to the state. The tax-dodger, no matter how high he may rate as a member of the church, is neither a good Christian nor a good citizen. I would not be willing to say that the good Christian may not take up arms in defense of home and country and those ideals and institutions which are most worth while. I am not ready to take the extreme position which many are taking to-day in regard to the Christian and war. But I am not ready to submit to the philosophy of the *Chicago Tribune:* "My country, may she ever be right; but right or wrong, my country." America is my country, whether she is right or wrong. I can go that far with the *Tribune.* But America is not my country to follow in a blind, dumb loyalty when my conscience and my God tell me it is in the wrong; but my country to redeem when it is wrong and try to make it right. And this is not a task for a cheap, flag-waving or professional patriotism, but for a patriotism which

willing to suffer, and die if need be, that its country
may be right instead of wrong on those great issues
which affect the life of the whole race.

We opposed Germany in the World War because
we regarded her treaties with Belgium as mere scraps
of paper. And while we were doing that, here in our
own America "all constitutional guarantees of free
assembly, free press, and free speech" were treated as
mere scraps of paper. "Nobody was allowed to think
or write or speak except according to orders. To dis-
courage conscription was to invite and insure persecution, imprisonment, death." (To dodge conscription
on the part of the rich, and those with a good political
pull, was an entirely different matter.) The man who
did not see eye to eye with a group of petty military
despots, who for some reason "were unavoidably de-
tained at home during the actual hostilities," was simply crushed by brute force. These acts were excused
and winked at because we were at war. Now the time
has come for all Christian citizens to repent and demand that our constitutional guarantees be treated as
something more than mere scraps of paper. Such a
nationalism as we see everywhere in America to-day
produces mere puppets rather than genuine patriots,
and great nations have never arisen out of the caution
and fear of puppets. Great nations have risen out of
the blood of real patriots—men who had a conscience
and dared to be true to it. The true law of patriotism
for the Christian is to be found in the "mind of Christ
rather than in the commands of the state." When
the followers of Jesus come to the place where they

cannot "render unto Cæsar" the things that he clair for his own without withholding from God "the thin that are God's," they must "obey God rather th men."

There is another thing which must be done. N tionalism at its best may be a beautiful thing. Ev with its faults, it represents the best attempt of m to live together and protect their common interests individuals and groups. We could not very well g on without the state. But as Christians we are und obligation to recognize the fact that the state has li itations. For the followers of Jesus the state cann approach perfection until it has become Christianiz until it has recognized the God who is above all hum governments. Speaking of the present attitude of t state, Dr. S. Parkes Cadman says: "Christians ha bowed in the house of Rimmon long enough. Toler tion of principles and practices which flatly contr dict the mind which was in Jesus Christ should e for his disciples here and now. The obdurate paga ism fed by tradition, temperament, education, and c lective sentiment has to be stoutly opposed as the mc formidable obstacle to the extension of God's kingdo to the safety of the nations, and to the welfare of ma kind. Whatever else is uncertain, this is certitude self, that if there is no restriction on national abs lutism Christ's governance ceases to be universal The Church must make nationalism Christian if eith or both of them are to survive. The Church may co tinue to exist as a religious society, perfectly harmle if Cæsar becomes God; but it cannot exist as a socie

70

f actual followers of Jesus Christ. When America
orgets the God of Jesus and exalts this modern con-
eption of the state above him, her doom will be
ealed. The state seems to have the final word to-day.
ut in reality, the last word belongs to Him who made
ossible all states, and is able to reverse the decisions
f the most powerful state men could ever build. The
ask of the Church will not be complete until "the
ingdoms of this earth become the kingdom of our
od and his Christ." And the price which modern
hristians must pay for their part in this conquest
ill be the same as the early Christians paid.

Out of that first great conflict between Christian-
y and nationalism there comes this story. The order
ad gone out that Christianity should be blotted out
f the empire, and especially out of the army. Every
oldier must bow before an image of the emperor and
our out a libation, or be put to death in any manner
hich his commander might choose. Up in northern
aul there was a band of one hundred men. Some of
hem were Christians, and they were the finest sol-
iers in the group. The officer in charge was sorry
hen he received the order; but he was obliged to
arry it out. He ordered his men to pass in single
le before the emblem of the emperor; and as they
assed, each man was to pour out his libation and
urn to the right. If he refused as a Christian, he
as to turn to the left. When the line had passed,
orty picked men had turned to the left—and death.
t was in the dead of winter, and the commander or-
ered these men to remove their clothing and march

to the middle of a frozen lake and there die from exposure. And as these men went they sang,

"Forty wrestlers, wrestling for Thee, O Christ,
    Claiming for Thee the victory and from Thee the crown."

This Roman officer, who was not a Christian, and who did not understand this strange religion which made men so loyal and so brave, caused a fire to be built on the shore of the lake hoping that his men might repent of their strange action and come back. He walked up and down in front of the fire listening to the song of the men as it came across the frozen water. Presently he saw one figure break away from the group and come stumbling across the ice and up the bank to the fire, choosing to save his life rather than be true to God. And then, this strong Roman's helmet and shield and uniform were thrown on the ground, and he walked out upon the ice to take the place of the traitor. And again the song went up to the skies, to be lost only in the silence of death,

"Forty wrestlers, wrestling for Thee, O Christ,
    Claiming for Thee the victory and for Thee the crown."

That type of allegiance and loyalty to God is unanswerable. Ancient Rome could not answer it and finally submitted to it. Thousands who looked upon the early Christians calmly going to their death for God became converts to Christianity. It was a Church with the courage to turn to the left for its conviction that won its first great victory over nationalism. In recent years, and especially during the World War, the Church here in America has not had the courage to turn to the left. It has turned to the right with the crowd and has poured out its libation of money and life upon the altar of the God of nationalism. And the results of this practice are evident. You may read them in the growing indifference of thousands of intelligent people toward organized religion; in half-empty church buildings all over the land; in the loss of membership in many of the great religious bodies; in the lack of faith in the genuineness of our religion by people in non-Christian lands; and in the fact that the Church has no commanding voice in the plans for the reconstruction of the world upon the basis of peace.

We cannot afford to ignore the fact, as one writer has put it, "that it was when Christianity was in the Catacombs as a despised and feared minority that it had its most glorious period in history. When it stopped being the faith of a minority, so deadly in earnest that they had to live underground, and became the superficial and conventional faith of the majority, the Church lost its distinctly Jesus-like character." The Church will not regain its power or find a voice which can speak with authority and command a hearing until it has the courage to turn to the left and pay the price, which may be the price of the cross. And for every traitor who deserts the Church for his own safety or comfort when it does make that turn, there will be some strong man to take his place and carry on. When the Church returns to God and again takes up his battle in earnest, the people will return to the Church.

73

WHEN COMETH THE END?

> *"And as he sat on the Mount of Olives, the disciples came unto him, privately, saying, Tell us, when shall these things be? and what shall be the sign of thy coming, and of the end of the world?"*
> MATTHEW 24: 3.

IV

WHEN COMETH THE END?

AS JESUS WENT OUT from the temple on the evening in which this question was asked, the thoughts in his mind about the temple, and the thoughts of the disciples, were very different. Like all loyal and devout Jews, the disciples were thrilled by the magnitude and the beauty of the temple buildings. To them, these buildings represented the last word in beauty, sacredness, and permanence. As a Jew, the temple meant all this to Jesus. But it meant infinitely more. As a careful student of the great prophets of his race, Jesus saw the spiritual significance of the temple and of Jerusalem as the holy city. And it was the fact that, for the vast majority of his people, the temple had lost its deep spiritual significance as the meeting place of God and man, and had become only the stronghold of a formal, dead religion, that challenged the thought of Jesus.

There before Jesus stood a magnificent pile of stones fashioned by the hands of men into exquisite loveliness, and upon the very "mountain of which it had been foretold that it should be at the head of all

77

the mountains, crowned with the house of God, the shining example to all nations of peace and true religion, the radiating center of divine justice for all the world.'' Jesus knew that Jerusalem had not fulfilled that high destiny and that the holy city was well-nigh past praying for. It had all but forfeited its right to be ''the focus of a nation's hope.'' Instead of shedding light upon a groping world ''its lifted mass loomed black and made life darker with its shadow.'' Rather than pointing men to God, it was ''shutting off heaven from earth and keeping men from God.'' It was while Jesus, in the loneliness of his own thoughts, was facing this ''ugly mass of accumulated selfishness and pride,'' that the disciples said, ''Master, behold, what manner of stones and what manner of buildings!'' And it was out of the deepest convictions of his own soul that the utter destruction of Jerusalem and the temple was inevitable, that he answered them: ''See ye not all these things? verily I say unto you, There shall not be left here one stone upon another, that shall not be thrown down.'' Jesus knew the disciples did not see the things which he saw in Jerusalem and the temple—the things which would make it a place of utter desolation. It was these words which called forth the question of the end of the world, a question which has been the subject of endless controversies through the centuries, and which is still a vital question for thousands of sincere and earnest followers of Jesus.

Jesus answered the question about the end of the world in what has been called his ''Discourse About

Last Things." This discourse is to be found in the thirteenth chapter of Mark, a part of the twenty-first chapter of Luke, and the twenty-fourth and twenty-fifth chapters of Matthew. The fact that it is filled with words and phrases "peculiar to the Jewish apocalypses" has presented a host of problems both for the scholars and the average readers of the New Testament. The questions which these words of Jesus raise are not easy to answer. Many of them can never be answered in an absolutely satisfactory manner, and one can easily spend more time pondering over them than is healthy for practical religious living. And yet they cannot be entirely ignored.

To the specific question of the disciples, "What shall be the sign of thy coming, and of the end of the world?" there appear to be three distinct answers. The first is very definite: "I tell you truly, this generation shall not pass away until all these things be accomplished." The second is entirely different and seemingly irreconcilable with the first: "No one knows of that day or hour, not even the angels in the heavens, nor the Son, only the Father." The third answer seems to be in agreement with the second: "And this gospel of the kingdom shall be preached in the whole world for a testimony unto all the nations: and then shall the end come."

Many attempts have been made to reconcile these answers one with the other. In the first, Jesus undoubtedly leaves the impression that the end is coming during the lifetime of that generation. There are sayings in other parts of the Gospels which leave the same

79

impression. In the other answers Jesus just as definitely leaves the impression that no one, not even himself, knew when the end was coming. In the last answer Jesus intimates very clearly that the chief business of his followers is "to preach the gospel of the kingdom" rather than to speculate about the end of the world. The great commission, as the Gospels report it, and Jesus' final words to his disciples as they are recorded in Acts, agree with this answer in putting the chief emphasis upon the preaching of the gospel. If we accept the first answer as that of Jesus, and we know that most of the first Christians did accept that answer, we are faced with the necessity of admitting that both Jesus and the first Christians were mistaken. If we accept the second and third answers, we have the weight of the Christian centuries on our side, and we know that toward the close of the first generation of Christians the hope that Jesus was coming immediately had already begun to wane. In the earliest letters of Paul the immediate coming of the Lord holds a prominent place. This is not so true of his later letters. When the second letter of Peter was written people were beginning to ask, "Where is the promise of his coming?" And the author gives this answer, which probably represents the answer of the Church to the growing skepticism concerning the end, "But forget not this one thing, beloved, that one day is with the Lord as a thousand years, and a thousand years as one day."

Scholars have sought a way out for those who do not like to believe that Jesus and the first Christians could have been mistaken. One solution is that in this discourse on last things and in those other passages which imply the immediate coming of the Lord, we do not have the words of Jesus, but only a "composite Jewish-Christian apocalypse" which has been inserted into the records by a later writer. Another is, that in all his references to the immediate return of the Son of Man in glory, Jesus was thinking of his own resurrection rather than the end of the world. Still another solution holds that this discourse contains two distinct narratives all mixed up together, the one having to do with the immediate destruction of Jerusalem and the temple, and the other with the final consummation of the Kingdom of God on earth. The first answer of Jesus belongs to the one narrative, and the second and third to the other. All of these solutions are suggestive, but none of them are entirely satisfactory.

We cannot get away from the fact that whatever Jesus said in answer to the disciples in this discourse on last things, his language was that of the age and the people to whom he was speaking. And that language is not the language of our Western and modern world. We do not accept the extreme point of view that the teachings of Jesus can only be understood in terms of eschatology; but we are quite sure that apart from eschatology we can never come to a full understanding of the message of Jesus. The real teachings of Jesus about the future have been obscured rather than illuminated by much of the technical discussion in the field of eschatology. Prof. Walter E. Bundy reveals a deep insight into this problem, and makes a much-needed contribution to thought in this field in this fine paragraph:

The eschatological form of Jesus' religious outlook is only a secondary matter. . . . It is at this point that both the eschatologists and the anti-eschatologists have committed grave error. The weakness of the position that sees in his thought eschatology only is that it condemns Jesus hopelessly to his own century and leaves him anchored there without a sure word for us to-day. Anti-eschatology is even weaker; it strips his thought of its characteristic forms, and leaves only shreds of his teachings, and it commits the gravest of historical errors by tearing Jesus from his own century. Eschatologists and anti-eschatologists alike miss, at least in theory, the tremendous religious faith of Jesus that expresses itself in this strange but natural form. Both have mistaken the characteristic for the essential; they have found the form and lost the content. . . . (Jesus') view of the future is essentially religious. The future, as he sees it and believes in it, is God's. It is of and from God. It is God and men in perfect society. . . . We must remember that there is nothing sacred in the spectacular scenery of Jesus' religious outlook. It is thoroughly characteristic of him and it may not be stripped from him as an historical figure, but it is never primary. The essential element in Jesus' view of the future is his faith in the fact that God has a kingdom, that it can and will come, and that soon, and that it is the highest calling of men to be worthy of it as their divine destiny. . . . This religious faith, announced with such great conviction and certainty, is the chief treasure which Jesus has in store for his followers. If we miss this, we have missed Jesus himself. Jesus was not committed unreservedly to the form of the future's realization, but to God who was to bring this future about.

A careful study of this whole "Discourse on Last Things," with these facts in mind, leaves one with the impression that the time and the manner of the coming of the end of the world was not the chief thing in the mind of Jesus. The bulk of the discourse is made up of warnings and admonitions to his disciples who are to take up the task of bringing about the realization of God's Kingdom on earth. This being true, the most satisfactory answer which Jesus gives to the questions of the disciples is that answer which is most vitally related to this task. Of many things, Jesus does not seem to be sure. But of one thing he speaks with positive conviction: "And the gospel of the kingdom shall be preached in the whole world for a testimony to all the nations; and then shall the end come." The destruction of Jerusalem, and with it the temple, might come within the lifetime of that present generation. But the final end, the consummation of all things, would not come until the gospel of the Kingdom had been preached so effectively that God and his Kingdom should prevail in the lives of men and of nations. Jesus makes it perfectly clear to the disciples that their business is not to speculate about the time or the manner of the coming of the end of the world, but to preach the gospel of the Kingdom in all the world. And in preparation for this task Jesus urged four very definite things upon his disciples. First, he warned them against false teachers: "Take heed that ye be not led astray: for many shall come in my name." Second, he warned them against fantastic and unhealthy interpretations of wars and those natural calamities which befall humanity regularly: "See that ye be not troubled: for these things must needs come to pass; but the end is not yet." Third, he warned them to guard carefully their own souls and be prepared to suffer for the kingdom: "But take heed unto yourselves: . . . in synagogues shall ye be beaten; . . . ye shall be hated of all men. . . . But he that endureth to the end, the same shall be saved." Fourth, Jesus urged upon his disciples the necessity for watchfulness at all times, "What I say unto you I say unto all, Watch." The chief burden of Jesus' message to the disciples seems to be in these practical warnings rather than in the highly figurative language which describes the coming of the end. Yet whole sections of the Church have often completely ignored this practical message in the attempt to interpret the other part of this discourse.

There are two general attitudes which modern Christianity may take concerning the second coming of Jesus and the end of the world. There is the attitude which expects the end may come at any time with Jesus appearing again in physical form. Those who hold to this view believe the consummation of the kingdom of God on earth will not come as the result of the "preaching of the gospel of the kingdom," but only through the direct intervention of Christ himself. According to this view the world is constantly getting worse rather than better, and it must continue to get worse until the end. There is nothing for the Church to do but save a few individuals out of the wreckage of the present world, and wait patiently for the end of all things. Some who accept this position believe that when Christ does come he will reign on earth for a thousand years before the final judgment. Others think the judgment will be immediate. The other attitude is that Jesus meant what he said when he sent his disciples out to preach the gospel of the kingdom to the ends of the earth; that the gospel is "the power of God unto salvation," both for individuals and nations, and that as the result of the faithfulness of the disciples in carrying out this commission and bearing witness to their Christ, the kingdom will come and the will of God be done on earth even as it is done in heaven. Those who accept this view believe that Christ is not only coming at the end of the world but is continually coming to keep his last great promise to the disciples, "Lo, I am with you always, even unto the end of the world."

The first attitude has been very popular since the World War. The belief in the immediate coming of the end has been revived during and following every great war. In some form, this view concerning the end of the world has been basic in the appeal of Fundamentalism to the world. It is not confined to a few fanatics or enthusiasts. The literal second coming of Christ is being preached by many perfectly orthodox and thoroughly sane evangelical ministers in our modern pulpits. Many churches are crowded by people who are eager to hear such a doctrine. A dozen Fundamentalist organizations within the great American religious bodies are committed to this position, and it is central in the message of the Dowieites, Russellites, and the Seventh-Day Adventists. This attitude is thoroughly pessimistic and fatalistic. The world is evil and is growing worse because this is God's plan. This view is based upon a literal and rather arbitrary interpretation of the Bible. Those who hold to this view specialize in doing the very things which Jesus warned his disciples not to do. They forget the real issues of the kingdom of God in their eagerness to prove that the world is to end at a certain time and that all who do not agree with them are enemies of God. They are so busy gazing into the heavens that they forget the earth upon which they stand and in which the gospel is to be preached. The preachers of this doctrine are sincere. But we are convinced that they are mistaken in their interpretation of the words of Jesus, and limited in their vision of the real significance of the kingdom of God as Jesus set forth that kingdom. Just so long as this doctrine is preached it will act as a brake on the wheels of progress and prove to be a serious obstacle in the way of the full realization of the kingdom of God on earth.

The real hope of the Church and the world lies along another road. The only attitude, it seems to me, which is wholly consistent with Jesus' conception of the kingdom of God, is this second attitude. We are here as Christians and as a Church, not to wait for the coming of the kingdom of God and the end of the world, but for the very definite purpose of helping to establish that kingdom. The hope of the speedy return of Jesus was very strong in the early Church. But while these Christians were looking for the coming of their Lord they were going everywhere preaching the gospel of the kingdom and literally turning their world upside down. The hope of the immediate coming of his Lord was strong in the soul of Paul, but it did not keep him from meeting all kinds of hardship for the sake of witnessing for Jesus before kings and preaching the gospel of the kingdom to the ends of his earth. The belief that Jesus might come at any time stimulated the early Christians to the task of preaching the gospel rather than breeding in them an utter hopelessness about the final triumph of the kingdom of God. Many of those things about which Jesus warned the disciples came to pass in the life of the early Church. His followers were hated and persecuted. They were brought before councils. Many of them suffered death. The story of the heroism of these early Christians is evidence of the fact that they had taken seriously the injunction of their Lord to watch, and were ready to meet death when it came. The story of Christianity through the centuries has reflected everything which Jesus mentions in his discourse on last things. And it has been the story of victory after victory which has been won by those who have set themselves to the task of preaching the gospel of the kingdom.

The primary task of the Church was in the beginning, is now, and always will be the "preaching of

87

the gospel of the kingdom'' to the ends of the earth. The kingdom has not come more speedily because very often the gospel which has been preached has been a one-sided gospel. The gospel Jesus preached, and that preached by the earliest Christian preachers, was an inclusive gospel. It included all that Jesus taught while he was on earth. And everything Jesus taught was given against the background of his ideal of the kingdom of God and its ultimate realization among men. The ideal life which is outlined in the Sermon on the Mount is to be the basis of citizenship in the kingdom. The parables were parables of the kingdom. The God of Jesus was the God whose will is to be done perfectly in the kingdom. It was God and his kingdom which filled the whole horizon of life and thought for Jesus. The "gospel of the kingdom" was a gospel of the reality of sin, for sin was the chief thing which stood in the way of the coming of the kingdom. It was a gospel of redemption, for only redeemed men could live up to the ideals of the kingdom. It was a gospel of human relationships, for it was in the kingdom that these relationships were to come to their perfection. It was a gospel of the future, a future which belonged to God and in which the souls of men will have an opportunity to expand to their fullest capacity.

If the early Church had confined its work to that of getting men and women ready to die, there would have been no clash with the Roman Empire. When it began to clear away the things which stood in the way

88

of the realization of the kingdom of God on earth, and to lay the foundations for that kingdom, it began to be recognized as a dangerous force in the empire. The Church can preach a one-sided and fragmentary gospel and not meet with very much opposition from the world. In fact, some fragmentary gospels have greatly pleased the worldly powers. But when the Church dares to preach the full gospel, "the gospel of the kingdom," it always finds itself in bitter opposition to the established order of things. But the end —the end of God's purpose for the race and the end of the world—will not come until all fragmentary gospels are discarded, all false prophets and Christs cast out, and the whole gospel, with all of its implications, both individual and social, is preached to all nations. It is idle to talk about the end of the world when this great task is as yet hardly begun.

In the picture of the last judgment, which is a part of Jesus' discourse on last things, the final inheritance is not for those who have simply watched for the coming of Jesus and the end of the world secure in their faith that the world must wax worse and worse until he does come. It is for those who have gone about the task of making the world a fit place for him when he does come by ministering to "the least of these" his brethren. Those who received the blessing of the Father were the people who had seen Jesus in the eyes of the needy of this earth and not coming on the clouds of heaven. Their eyes had been upon the earth with its suffering and need rather than upon the heavens. Those who went out from the presence of Jesus in that judgment scene with his words of condemnation ringing in their ears were simply the people who had not seen him in the garb of suffering and needy humanity. The final test for us as Christians will not be whether we have seen Jesus coming in the clouds of glory, but whether we have seen him in those clouds of human need which hover about us all the time. In those scenes in the book of Revelation you will remember that the crowns are reserved for those whose robes had been dyed red in the blood of suffering and persecution with and for their Lord, rather than for those who have stood and waited in robes of spotless white for the coming of their Lord. Jesus may come some day on the clouds of glory. I would not take that hope away from a single soul. But the Jesus the Church needs, and the Jesus our world needs, is this Jesus who is actually coming in clouds of human need and glory all the time.

Edwin Markham has a poem which is based upon an incident in our early American history. When the famous Dark Day of 1780 came upon New England, a group of senators wanted to rush from their meeting place to the house of God to pray. They were halted by one of their number who said, as the poet has put it:

> "Bring in the lights: let us be found
> Doing our duty's common round.
> Bring in the candles: keep to the task;
> What more can judgment angels ask?"

What more can Jesus ask of his Church when he does come than this? What would please him more than to find his Church consecrating all its strength, and power, and resources to the task of preaching "the gospel of the kingdom" to all the nations?

WHICH COMMANDMENT IS GREATEST?

"Teacher, which is the greatest commandment in the law?"

Matthew 22: 36.

V
WHICH COMMANDMENT IS GREATEST?

WHEN THE PHARISEES HEARD that Jesus had completely routed and silenced the Sadducees with their foolish question about the resurrection, they sent one of their own number, a lawyer, to tempt him with the question about the greatest commandment. The scribes and the Pharisees put so much emphasis upon the commandments of their religion that the discussion as to which was the greatest of these commandments was a very common one. Their codes of ethics and morals were very complex, and they were often hard pressed in their efforts to answer the questions which they raised in the minds of the people. Although Jesus was aware of the motive in the mind of this lawyer, he gave this question the consideration which so great a question deserved. He did not argue with his questioner. His answer was short and directly to the point. "Thou shalt love the Lord thy God with all thy heart, and with all thy soul, and with all thy mind. This is the first and great commandment. And the second is like unto it, Thou shalt love thy neighbor as thyself. On these two commandments hang all the law and the prophets.''

This reply, as Dr. Erdman has so well said, ''is startling in its insight and simplicity; he declares that the whole duty of man, the full sum of moral obligation, the essence of all divine law, is embodied and expressed in the word 'love.' This love must be exercised in two directions, first toward God, and second toward men. All the Ten Commandments and all other divine requirements are but expressions of this one supreme principle.'' During the last week Jesus gave to his disciples what he called a new commandment: ''A new commandment I give unto you, that ye love one another.'' Thus, in the mind of Jesus, ''the greatest commandment,'' both in the religion of his fathers and in his own religion, was simply this— ''Thou shalt love.''

The manifestation of this love was to be three-fold. The up-reach of this greatest commandment was to be toward God: ''Thou shalt love God.'' The in-reach of this greatest commandment was to be toward the members of the Christian community: ''Thou shalt love one another.'' The out-reach of this greatest commandment was to be toward others: ''Thou shalt love thy neighbor.'' In the parable of the Good Samaritan which Luke gives as a part of the answer of Jesus to this same question earlier in his ministry, Jesus makes it perfectly clear that a neighbor is the man who plays the rôle of the Good Samaritan along the highways of life, and that our neighbors are those of our less fortunate fellows who are lying along those highways in need of our help. There are two neighbors in this parable—the man who acted like a neighbor ought to act, and the man who was a neighbor because of his helplessness and need. As a matter of convenience we shall think of this greatest commandment under three divisions, but in reality we shall see how utterly impossible it is to separate these three manifestations. They belong together.

"Thou shalt love the Lord thy God with all thy heart, and with all thy soul, and with all thy mind." Jesus had nothing to add to this commandment. But he had a conception of God, a revelation of the nature of God, to offer to men which has made it much easier for them to keep this commandment. Before men can love God with their whole being they must be convinced that God is worthy of such love. This is the supreme assumption of the New Testament about God—that he is a God worthy to be loved by all men, and that he inspires in men, when they actually come to know him, a desire to love him. The God of the Old Testament did not always inspire love in the hearts of men. The Old Testament writers urged men to "fear God and keep his commandments," and very often fear and love were confused one with the other. The God of Jesus, and of the New Testament, is a God whom men may love without being afraid in the sense in which fear was generally used in the Old Testament. He is not the far-away God of the Jews, the angry Judge upon the bench, or the all-powerful Monarch upon his throne, but the loving Father whose interests are with his children here on earth. When

Jesus talked about God men felt that he was near. It was perfectly natural for them to look into his face as it was reflected in Jesus, and to love him and call him Father. In the mind of the New Testament writers God was not only love in his very essence and nature, but he was continually manifesting that love toward man.

Jesus was supremely concerned about the in-reach of love. Three times during that last evening with his disciples he urged them to love one another. "A new commandment I give unto you, that ye love one another. . . . This is my commandment, that ye love one another. . . . These things I command you, that ye love one another." In the mind of Jesus the badge of discipleship was to be love. "By this shall all men know that ye are my disciples, if ye have love one for another." The early Christians took this command of Jesus seriously. They were not perfect in their practice of this love, but they never entirely ignored it. The apostles laid much stress upon the necessity of love. Paul urged the Christians at Ephesus to "walk in love," and to the Romans he wrote, "Be kindly affectioned one to another with brotherly love." To the church at Corinth where there were grave abuses in connection with the use of spiritual gifts and where there was an unwholesome excitement over the gift of tongues, Paul points to love as "the more excellent way." All those other gifts which belong to Christians, and which are necessary to the life and growth of the Christian community, become empty and meaningless, Paul says, when they are exercised

98

at the expense of love. He does not attempt to say what Christian love is, but he is sure of what it does, of how it works in action. "Love is very patient, very kind. Love knows no jealousy: love makes no parade, gives itself no airs, is never rude, never selfish, never irritated, never resentful; love is never glad when others go wrong, love is gladdened by goodness, always slow to expose, always eager to believe the best, always hopeful, always patient." (Moffatt.) And when all these other gifts over which men dispute at the expense of love have disappeared, love will last on, for "it is the greatest of all."

The chief burden of John's message to the early Church, as we have it in his letters, is that the followers of Jesus should love each other. "He that loveth his brother abideth in the light. . . . But he that hateth his brother is in darkness, and walketh in darkness. For this is the message which we have heard from the beginning, that we should love one another. . . . Beloved, let us love one another, for love is of God: and everyone that loveth is born of God, and knoweth God. . . . And this is the commandment we have from him, that he who loveth God love his brother also." According to John, Christians were to know that they were Christians by the measure of their love one for the other. "We know that we have passed from death unto life, because we love the brethren. He that loveth not his brother abideth in death." And for John, love was to be the mark of discipleship by which the world might know the followers of Jesus. "In this the children of God are manifest, and the

99

children of the devil: whosoever doeth not righteousness is not of God, neither he that loveth not his
brother.'' The first Christian community was a community of lovers, and those evils which received the
most severe condemnation at the hands of the apostles
were the ones which marred or destroyed love.

The out-reach of love was one of the chief foundation stones of the kingdom of God as Jesus con-
ceived it. He knew that this kingdom could never be
realized until men loved their neighbors. Until the
love of mankind embraced all men as neighbors, the
will of God could not be done as perfectly on earth as
it was in heaven. Jesus met his greatest difficulties
and encountered his greatest opposition when he urged
men to face all the implications of this out-reach of
love. The commandment to love one's neighbor was
old when Jesus was born. It was recognized as one
of the greatest of all the commandments. But in the
hands of the Jews it had been interpreted in such a
way that it became practically meaningless. So long
as a man can decide for himself just who his neighbor
is, this commandment does not become so difficult.
This is exactly what the Jew had done. The neighbors
had been narrowed down to a select few. In the parable of the Good Samaritan Jesus challenged this nar-
rowness. He removed all restrictions. He no longer
left the matter to the judgment of the individual. A
man's neighbor was not some particular individual
whom he wanted to love, but any man, every man,
anywhere on the face of the earth who was in need.

100

It was this removal of all restrictions on neighborliness which brought Jesus into conflict with the Jews.

Jesus went further than his own people in his emphasis upon the out-reach of love. To the neighbor of the religion of his fathers, who was to be the out-reach of love, he added the enemy. In his religion men were to love both their enemies and their neighbors. "Ye have heard that it hath been said, Thou shalt love thy neighbor and hate thine enemy. But I say unto you, Love your enemies, bless them that curse you, do good to them that hate you, and pray for them that despitefully use you, and persecute you." The saying of Jesus about loving one's enemy was a hard one for his age to comprehend. The religion of the Jews did not ignore a man's duties toward his enemies. In the book of Exodus we find this injunction, "If thou meet thine enemy's ox or his ass going astray, thou shalt surely bring it back to him again." We find this word in Proverbs: "Rejoice not when thine enemy falleth, and let not thine heart be glad when he stumbleth. . . . If thine enemy be hungry, give him bread to eat; if he be thirsty, give him water to drink." These passages reflect the higher level of thought among the Jews; but so far as their actual practice was concerned, the words of Jesus were a more accurate statement of the facts—"Thou shalt love thy neighbor and hate thine enemy." The history of his people, as Jesus knew it, was filled with hatred rather than love toward the enemy. He had come to point men toward a new way. He knew where

101

the path of hate had led his nation. He knew where the path of love would lead.

The early Church put much emphasis upon this out-reach of love. Paul urged the Roman Christians to love their neighbors as themselves. To the Galatians he wrote, "For all the law is fulfilled in one word, even in this: Thou shalt love thy neighbor as thyself." James says, "If ye fulfil the royal law, according to the scripture, Thou shalt love thy neighbor as thyself." This church won its way into many communities by its practice of neighborliness. In fact, the church did not think much about any permanent organization until its benevolent work became a heavy burden upon the shoulders of the apostles. This benevolence began within the Christian community, but it did not stay there long. The poor, the needy, the common slave, and even the temple prostitutes were looked upon as subjects of neighborliness; and as these people whom the other religions of the empire had ignored and passed by came into a new manhood and womanhood in Jesus Christ, the pagan world began to take notice. When Christianity began to bind up the wounds of those who had been bruised and beaten by the heartless paganism of the first-century world, it began its age-long conquest over the hearts of men.

"Thou shalt love" has always been the supreme commandment in the Christian Church. It is the greatest of all the commandments in the religions of the world. All religions have given it in some form or another, but only Christianity has given the dynamic which makes its ultimate realization possible.

"Thou shalt love God." We need to urge that upon the modern world. But before we can urge men to love God we must be sure we have a God to present to them whom they can love and will want to love. The God of our traditional Christian theology has not always been a God who inspires love in men. Many of our conceptions of God which have been thoroughly orthodox, and which are still being preached from some pulpits and in some books, are repulsive to the modern mind and heart. A God who would be a party to some of the traditional schemes of the atonement would not measure up to our common ethical standards to-day. There is no place in the modern mind or heart for a God who would send unbaptized infants to a hell of fire and brimstone, and there could be little respect to-day for a God who arbitrarily condemns a certain portion of the race to hell and reserves heaven for a few of the elect, who are elect not because of anything which they have believed or done, but simply because God has selected them. Men might have feared the God of Augustine and Calvin at one time, but they will not love him to-day. Because men have refused to love, or even believe in such a God as this, many substitutes have been offered. And yet, when we look carefully at the whole list of modern gods which are being worshiped by many people, we do not find one who commands the love of men in the sense in which the greatest commandment urged men to love God. Men may respect, and even fear, that impersonal force which we are told created and holds the universe together, but they will not love it. They are more inclined to curse it than love it. Our modern gods are not lovable gods. The injunction to love God falls upon heedless ears unless there is a God who can be loved.

If we expect men to love God to-day, we must make them sure of the God of Jesus. For Jesus, personality, in the form of a Father who is interested in his children, is at the heart of the universe. "I do not know," says one who is searching for God, "what God is. I go to the theologians, and what they say confuses rather than enlightens. . . . But in the dark I turn to God in the simplest, best ways men have found for bringing him near and making him real; I call him Father, as Jesus tells me to do: and the light shines." There is no uncertainty and caprice about this Father-God of Jesus, and in his very essence he is love. Men come to love him because he has first loved men with a love which begets love. Once we are persuaded that God really loves us, the rest of our religion will follow in a natural way. In all the relationships of life this God becomes the constant, the trustworthy factor. And this God of Jesus is a seeking God. There is only one meaning to the fifteenth chapter of Luke—that men are the children of God and he is constantly seeking their welfare and salvation. The love of God which is pictured here is a love which will never rest until the lost is found. The older theologians tried to reduce or expand Jesus to their measure of God. The new theology, the genuinely Christian theology, begins with Jesus and seeks to interpret God in terms of his revelation of God and his own religious experience of God. And the God we see in the face of Jesus Christ is the only God men can ever really love.

A sadly divided and bewildered Church is evidence of the fact that the in-reach of love has not been practiced among the followers of Jesus as it should have been. No single commandment in the Christian religion has been so consistently ignored and repudiated by the Church in its long history as Jesus' commandment that Christians should love one another. Dr. Charles E. Jefferson bears testimony to the fact that during one of the longest ministries ever held in America, he never found a single "applicant for church membership worried about his inability to keep the new commandment." People, he points out, "do not measure their fitness to become members of the Christian Church by their willingness to obey this new commandment." And Dr. Jefferson puts the blame for this situation upon the shoulders of the theologians and preachers. "I have recently looked through two hundred volumes of modern sermons," he says, "and have found only one sermon on the new commandment, and that one was preached by a preacher who has been dead for over seventy years. . . . The theologians have never been interested in this commandment. The Christian scholars most revered have never taken time to explore the meaning of it. The theologians have busied themselves with the doctrines in the historic creeds, and the historic creeds knew nothing of the new commandment. No congregations have been trained in any land to repeat Sunday after

105

Sunday, 'I believe in the new commandment. I believe in loving my fellow-Christians even as Christ loved us.' " What Jesus made primary the Church has often made secondary, and what he made secondary the Church has made primary. The blackest chapters in the history of Christianity, chapters which reveal how men have been persecuted and burned in the name of religion because their beliefs did not square with the beliefs of the Church, would never have been written if the Church had taken this in-reach of love seriously. Because the Church has failed to love within its own walls and fellowship, the world is not yet convinced that those who call themselves Christians are really followers of Jesus Christ. When the Church substituted "credo" for "amo" as the test of fellowship, it ceased to be genuinely Christian. When it takes this new commandment seriously enough to act upon it, the vision of the poet will be realized:

"The hour is coming when the walls of the present Church
Shall melt away, and in its stead shall rise a nobler Church,
Whose covenant word shall be the deeds of love.
Not Credo then, Amo shall be the password through its gates.
Man shall not ask his brother any more, Believest Thou? but,
　　Lovest Thou?
And all shall answer at God's altar, Lord, I love.

For hope may anchor, faith may steer,
But love, great love alone, is captain of the soul."

The Church has not always practiced the outreach of love as Jesus urged it upon his followers.

106

Christians have not loved their neighbors as they should, surely not as they have loved themselves. Rather, in our modern acquisitive society, because of love for self, and a desire to be surrounded by the comforts and luxuries of life, Christians have often exploited their neighbors for gain and left them half dead by the side of the road. The Jericho road runs clear around the earth, and it is very modern. It has always been lined with neighbors. Millions of men are still lying by the side of the road, beaten and half dead at the hands of that glorified robber called war. The modern Jericho road is lined with the victims of the slums of our great cities—men, women, and little children who have been sacrificed to that other popular robber called greed. And everywhere, on all the highways of the world, we find the wrecks of our present industrial system—human wrecks, the broken bodies of men who have been cast aside as so much useless machinery. There are literally millions of neighbors in the world to-day waiting for the Church to play the rôle of the Good Samaritan. The tragedy is the fact that thousands of our modern Christians in their comfortable homes and beautiful churches do not even recognize these victims of our modern civilization as having any neighborly claims upon the Church.

And modern Christianity has not yet met the test of the out-reach of love in its attitude toward the enemy. Incredible as it all seems since we have had time to think it over, we know that during the World War in practically all of the so-called Christian nations the churches were centers of hate rather than love. And the hatred which was generated during those awful years is still in the blood of the nations, blocking at every turn the pathway toward peace. Until the Church is able to release within its own life that love which is greater than hate, that power which will enable it actually to follow Jesus all the way in his attitude toward the enemy, it cannot release that power in the life of the world.

"Here is a little creed,
Enough for all the roads we go.
In love is all the law we need,
In Christ is all the God we know."

WHAT IS TRUTH?

"What is truth?"
                    JOHN 18: 38.

VI

WHAT IS TRUTH?

JESUS WAS ON TRIAL in the judgment hall of Pilate. "Art thou the King of the Jews?" asked Pilate. Jesus answered: "Sayest thou this thing of thyself, or did others tell it of me?" The answer seemed to irritate Pilate. "Am I a Jew?" he asked. "Thine own nation and the chief priests have delivered thee unto me: what hast thou done?" And Jesus answered: "My kingdom is not of this world." "If you are not the King of the Jews, then, are you a king at all?" demanded Pilate. To this question Jesus replied: "Thou sayest that I am a king. To this end was I born, and for this cause came I into the world, that I should bear witness unto the truth." Then Pilate asked: "What is truth? And when he had said this, he went out again unto the Jews, and saith unto them, I find in him no fault at all."

We will never know all that was in the mind of Pilate when he asked this question, or why he did not remain for an answer. And we will never know just what answer Jesus would have given to that question had Pilate remained. There have been some interest-

ing guesses. Lord Bacon's words, "What is truth?
said jesting Pilate, and would not stay for an answer,"
have become almost as well known as the words of
Pilate himself. Most careful students of the Gospels,
however, have failed to agree with Bacon's judgment
of Pilate. Frederick W. Robertson, in his famous
sermon on *The Skepticism of Pilate,* Dr. W. M. Clow,
in his interesting study of Pilate in *The Day of the
Cross,* and Dr. J. D. Jones, in his thoughtful discussion of Pilate's attitude toward Jesus—all agree that
Pilate was in no mood for jesting when he asked that
question. Uncertainty was there, and possibly a touch
of sarcasm, but the question was not asked in the
spirit of the jester. Pilate had never found the truth
for himself, and he was suspicious of all those who
claimed to have discovered the truth. "Pilate's question breathed of hopelessness. He felt that Jesus was
unjustly condemned, but he thought in his views as
hopelessly wrong as all the rest; all were wrong. What
was truth? Who knows anything about it? He spoke
too bitterly, too hopelessly, too disappointedly to get
an answer." This is the judgment of Robertson.
"What is truth? It was the partly impatient, partly
contemptuous, partly despairing word of a man who
flings out a question to which he conceives there is no
answer at all. . . . There is no word to describe Pilate
but one, and that is Agnostic." This is Dr. Clow's
conclusion. Dr. Jones concludes that the question is
that of a cynic. "The age in which Pilate lived was a
skeptical age. Faith in the old religions had disappeared and no new and better faith had come to take

their place. The old pagan worships were still main-
tained, but the cultured part of mankind had ceased to
believe in them. They knew they were not true. And
further, not only had there been this decay of faith,
but there were certain schools of philosophers who
doubted the reality of knowledge. They challenged
the validity of the evidence of the senses. They denied
the possibility of knowing a thing in itself. The result was that amongst the educated people the spirit
of skepticism was almost universal. . . . Pilate was an
agnostic, and it is the cynical, bitter, disillusioned
temper of the agnostic that breathes through this question, 'What is truth?' "

Just how Jesus would have answered this question had Pilate waited for the answer, we do not know.
Perhaps he would not have answered it at all. But we
do know at least a part of what Jesus might have said
by what he did say about truth. The statements of
Jesus about truth are not many, but they are reveal-
ing. "I am the truth. . . . The words which I speak
unto you, they are truth, and they are life. . . . To this
end was I born, and for this cause came I into the
world, that I should bear witness unto the truth. . . .
If ye continue in my word, then ye are my disciples
indeed; and ye shall know the truth, and the truth
shall make you free." From these statements it is
evident that Jesus did not ignore the question about
truth. He assumed that in the realm where he lived
and thought truth was knowable—"Ye shall know the
truth." This truth which was knowable could be
known through him—"I am the truth." And this truth

113

which may be known through Jesus himself and his words is a liberating force in the life of men and in the life of the race. These are the fundamental assumptions of Jesus as he faces the question about truth.

Jesus was not interested in truth in the abstract. He said nothing about the value of what philosophers call "pure thought." He was not interested in that truth which "is beaten out and condensed in creeds" and systems of thought for the acceptance and use of men. He knew how ineffectual this kind of truth had been in the life of his people. The truth which made hypocrites out of its self-appointed guardians was repulsive to Jesus. His interest was in truth "as it proceeds from the heart of God, and is worked into the warp and woof" of the everyday life of men. Robertson holds that Jesus used the term "truth" as being the equivalent of "reality." "For truth, substitute reality," he says, "and it will become more intelligible." Jesus' life "was a witness to the truth in the sense of reality. The reality of life—the reality of the universe—to these his every act and word bear testimony. His life corresponded with reality as the dial with the sun. His very being here manifested to the world Divine reality." For Jesus, "truth was something very tangible, workable, and livable," and he lived the truth so effectively that he did not need to talk much about it.

It was this truth, this reality at the heart of life and the universe, which Jesus assumed was knowable. All that men needed to know about God and them-

Definition

114

selves and life could be known. "There is nothing covered that shall not be revealed: and hid that shall not be known. . . . Unto you it is given to know the mysteries of the kingdom of God." Here we have a sublime faith in the knowableness of God's universe which the greatest men of science have never surpassed. According to Jesus we do not live in a universe where the truth forever evades us; but in a universe in which the truth shall be known. Against the background of the religion of his fathers in which truth had become a static thing confined to systems and dogmas, in the midst of a world of pagan philosophy which was skeptical of all truth, and surrounded by innumerable "cults of mystery and sacrament which traded in the unknowable and exalted trance above reason," Jesus promised men that they would at last be able to see their way "through all the wonders of the whole wide realm of God; and it is the promise of a thinker who does not use words without feeling their meaning, who understands the appeal of God and his ways." Because Jesus assumed that truth was knowable he urged his followers to be seekers after the truth. All the truth they had known was that which they had accepted from the religious leaders of their day. "Seek, and ye shall find; knock, and it shall be opened unto you," said Jesus. He would have his disciples become truth-seekers rather than mere truth-accepters. Some of our modern truth-seekers may ignore Jesus because his Church has not always followed him in his search for truth. This has been one of great tragedies of Christian history. But

115

the truth-seekers of any age will not launch out upon any trail where they will not find the marks of Jesus of Nazareth and his living spirit just a little ahead of them. No matter what attitude his Church has taken or may take toward truth, Jesus belongs with the truth-seekers of the race.

The truth which Jesus assumed could be known, and which he urged men to seek, is knowable through his life and words. "I am the truth. . . . The words that I speak unto you, they are truth. . . . If ye abide in my word, ye shall know the truth." No other religious teacher ever talked like that. Here are the most tremendous claims any man ever made for himself and his message. And yet they stand after nineteen hundred years of human history in which whole systems of thought and civilization have come and gone, with the verdict of the best thought and life of the race in their favor. In the presence of the ultimate realities of life and the universe, the life and message of Jesus of Nazareth remain unequaled and unsurpassed. It is utterly impossible to separate the life and words of Jesus. In some cases it makes the words of men more important when we can separate them from the lives of their authors, for the authors of great and helpful words have very often lived very unworthy lives. The words of Jesus become meaningless when we try to separate them from his life. His words are truth because they issued from a life which was truth. His life was truth because it is the only life which we know anything about which was perfectly at home among the deepest realities of God's universe. His

116

words are true because they deal with the deepest realities men know anything about. His life was truth because it was reality itself.

Joseph Fort Newton holds that Jesus' utterance, "I am the truth," is "the most remarkable utterance that ever fell from human lips. It is either arrogance or sublimity; sheer nonsense or fathomless profundity. He does not say that he is a teacher of the truth, but that he is the truth; not all truth, but the highest truth; the truth that men most want to know—the truth that makes all other truth true." In every century since Jesus lived men have attempted to prove that Jesus and his message were outside of truth, that the world of thought had entirely outgrown them. The twentieth century is not the only century in which men have written about the "twilight of Christianity." There are whole systems of thought in our modern world in which Jesus and his message have no place. And yet the heart of the world continues to turn to Jesus and his words for that truth without which it cannot live. Truth was made for the heart as well as for the head, and the weakness of much that passes for truth in the modern world is that it has forgotten that man has a heart.

In Jesus and his words we find the truth concerning those ultimate things which man wants to know about, and must know about to live—God, man, the meaning and purpose of life here, and the question of life after death. Jesus was the truth about God—a God who knows, and cares, and loves; a God from whose love men can never be separated by any of the experiences or circumstances of life or by the fact of physical death itself; a Father who can be trusted, who suffers when his children go astray, who seeks them when they are lost, and in whose house there is a place for them when they decide to come back home. Jesus brought the "far-off God of the Jews" near to all men, and the "unknowable God" of the philosopher, the skeptic and the agnostic, he made knowable in terms of personality. Jesus was the truth about man—the truth that man is a child of this Father-God; a child capable of thinking God's thoughts after him, of working with God, and of infinite development and perfection. Jesus knew all the ugly, black things which have found lodgment in the human heart. But he knew there was something in men which is great, that the "raw-stuff of humanity" is touched with the divine, and he thought of men, not in terms of what they were, but in terms of what they were capable of becoming when the truth of God and the sacredness of their own natures flooded their minds and hearts. Before man at his worst and lowest, Jesus held the ideal of man at his highest and best, with the unshakable conviction that the ideal could and would be realized.

Jesus was the truth about life and its meaning and purpose. He believed that life could be infinitely great, and that human personality was the supreme channel through which God was working out his purpose for the universe. "A man's life," Jesus declared, "consisteth not in the abundance of the things which he possesseth." To those who were making of life just one wild scramble for material possessions, he

118

said, "Seek ye first the kingdom of God and his righteousness, and all these things shall be added unto you."
Jesus pointed out the unpleasant truth that the man
whose chief aim in life had been to lay up enough
wealth so that his soul could take its ease, was a fool
in the sight of God. Life, in the thought of Jesus, was
to be an abundant thing and always sacrificial. Life
was of more value than the whole material world, and
the bargain in which a man traded his whole life for
material possessions was without profit. And Jesus
was the truth about that life which is eternal. For
Jesus, all life was "eternal life." He never tried to
prove the reality of eternal life. Because God was
what he was for Jesus, and because man was what he
was, and life on this earth was what it was—he assumed the immortality of the soul and the endlessness
of life for the children of God. For Jesus, because
God was the God of the living rather than the God of
the dead, eternal life was sure. Jesus' idea of eternal
life was not a doctrine by itself; it was implied in all
that he said and did while he was on earth. It was a
part of that truth which he was and to which his
whole life witnessed while he was among men.

It was this truth, which was to be knowable
through himself and his words, that Jesus declared
would make all men free. Only when men know the
truth about God are they free from those supersti-
tions and false religions which keep them in bondage
to the half-gods or the hopelessly limited gods. Not
until men know the truth about the ultimate reality
which is at the heart of the universe will they begin

to live as those who are at home in the universe. Not until men know the truth about themselves will they begin to act like sons of God. Jesus came, says one of the greatest of the apostles, "to bring life and immortality to light." He came to rediscover men to themselves, to make them feel that the "divine urge" which they experience in the higher moods of the soul is not the mockery of their imaginations and emotions, but the actual life of God seeking to express itself in them. He came to make men realize that the only chains which can bind them and keep them from the final realization of their destiny as sons of God, are the chains which they themselves have made, and that only through the coöperation of their wills with the Divine will can those chains ever be broken. Not until men come to realize the truth that the human soul can never be satisfied with the abundance of mere things, will they be freed from those false philosophies of life and those false economic theories and systems which make them slaves to things. And not until men know the truth that death does not end all, will they be free from the terrors of death and the grave.

What is truth? According to Jesus and the New Testament, it is something which may be known through Jesus and his words, and something which, when it is known, makes men free. Jesus did not say that this or that particular thing was truth. But the follower of Jesus knows, when he stands in the presence of that which has the marks of reality upon it and which is actually liberating human life and making it nobler, he is standing in the presence of truth. He knows when he surveys those moral and social forces which are making the world a better place in which to live, and which are enriching and uplifting human life as a whole, he is looking upon truth. And when he comes to grips with that belief which causes men and women absolutely to refuse, in the face of all the facts which point in the other direction, to hopelessly leave their dead in the grave—he is convinced beyond the shadow of a doubt that he is moving in the realm of ultimate truth.

It is this truth which Christianity has to offer the world—the truth which is in Jesus and his teachings. Our age is not unlike that age in which Pilate lived. Doubt is widespread, and very deeply rooted in the minds of many people. Atheism—a militant atheism which not only denies the God of Christianity but all other gods, and the very possibility of humanity ever knowing any god—is very popular. A deep-seated skepticism concerning man himself is also having a mighty influence over the modern mind. The "Modern Temper," as Joseph Wood Krutch and others describe it for us, is a temper and mood which refuses to see any value in anything at all. All is black. All we have cherished as truth is either fiction or falsehood. Truth is forever beyond our grasp, and man would be better off if he had never reached that stage of consciousness which caused him to ask questions about himself and his destiny. We are completely disillusioned with the laboratory, love is a value which is dead, life and art and peace are prostrate, and the certitudes of religion and philosophy are mere phantoms. It is against this

121

background and in the face of this despairing mood that we are, as Christians, to present Jesus and his message as the one truth which is knowable and which can actually liberate the souls of men.

It is this truth which our age needs. Science asks us to be patient and wait for that truth which can be verified in the laboratory. Philosophy asks us to wait until all the facts are in before we demand the truth. But life itself demands the truth here and now. As Rabbi Silver has pointed out in his brilliant book on *Religion in a Changing World,* there is some truth we cannot wait for. "Mankind cannot now wait until the slow accumulation of verifiable knowledge shall give warrant for a desperately needed philosophy of life. Each generation must live its life—and its life is short. It cannot wait until all the facts are in and all the data collected." After all, the very facts which are so desperately needed for a satisfactory philosophy of life, have not yet been and may never be verified in the laboratory of the scientist or the study of the philosopher. Men may live very satisfactory lives without knowing anything about Aristotle or William James or John Dewey. They may, as Dr. Jones says, "live a noble life without knowing anything about astronomy or geology . . . or atoms or electrons. Millions do live quite happily without knowing anything about them, and most of us manage pretty well without knowing much." A man may be honest enough to be trusted in a great bank without knowing all the secrets of the laboratory, and a man who is not at home in the physical sciences may be an expert in the science of government. But no man can be happy and trusted and useful and live a really abundant life who does not know something about those ultimate truths which have to do with God, himself, the meaning and purpose of life, and the final destiny of the human soul. When men are careless of, indifferent toward, or wrong about any of these fundamental truths, they do not make the best citizens of any community or the kind of human beings who make the world better.

Only the God of Jesus can answer man's deepest questions about ultimate reality. The gods of science and philosophy will not do. The "unknowables" of the skeptic and the agnostic and the "no-gods" of the atheists will pass with the passing mood and temper of our age. But the human heart, which still "pants for the living God" even as it did in the days of the shepherd-poet, will last on. And when that heart pauses in the silence of a great loneliness or breaks over the tragedy of a great sorrow, blind, heartless, Force, or "a stream of Tendency making for righteousness," cannot speak the words of courage and comfort which are needed. In the supreme hours of the human soul men want to see the face of a Father reflected in the face of Jesus Christ. They want a God who is as near and as real as the handclasp of a friend in the dark. The present hopeless and despairing views of man will not meet the tests of man's deepest experiences. Only the revelation of Jesus that life is noble; that in spite of his sin and inclination to wander into the far-country and waste much of that precious stuff out of which life is made in living below the level of his manhood, he is a child of the Father, belongs in the Father's house, and has the power of will to say, "I will arise and go to my Father"—only this will satisfy the deepest needs and the highest moods of the soul.

Man will never be permanently satisfied with mere things any more than the prodigal was satisfied with the husks in the far-country. "A tray full of mechanical toys, or engines and motors and radios," or a bank full of silver and gold and stocks and bonds cannot feed the souls of men. Years ago, in one of his most striking essays, J. Brierley pointed out the folly of those who were trying to dispense with the spiritual realities of life. "Men have," he said, "made experiments in two directions: in that of the intellect and that of the senses. They have both been failures. Science, with all the secrets it unlocks, has not yet stumbled on the secret of happiness. We are still trying hard at the other experiment, that of the senses. Wealth is the minister of the senses, and ours is the age of millionaires. But in our rage for money we have forgotten to inquire as to its purchasing power. It can buy you houses, lands, furniture, Lucullus banquets—in fact, world, flesh, and devil. But in your luxurious hotel, as you drink the champagne and order about the obsequious waiters, and receive the homage of those who make their profit in you, you discover that there is a class of things not contained in the menu, and which all the resources of the manager cannot procure for you. It is that class of things by which the soul lives. Those invisibles we call love, joy, peace,

124

temperance, meekness, faith; the commodities known
as fidelity, comradeship, trust; the disciplines by which
man becomes conscious of his best self, of the Divine
in him and around him; these are the articles with
which neither your banker nor your hotel manager
can supply you. . . . And yet without these things you
are miserable.'' Those of us who are seeing science
beginning to admit that it has promised a bigger order
than it can deliver, and who have witnessed the house
of wealth crashing upon the shoulders of many of its
builders, know the truth of these words. When men
are soul-hungry, they instinctively turn toward the
Father's house.

The modern world will never be satisfied with a
mere negation in the presence of death. In the end,
nothing but the truth as we have it in Jesus will do.
''For he is a Christ who has died and is alive again.
He taught us in words that God is the God of the living and not of the dead. But he did not leave it there.
He himself died, and then after he died he came back
again just to make us sure that there are sweet fields
beyond the swelling flood. Plato guessed about immortality, but it is Jesus who makes us sure. He is
the truth. The answer to all the heart's queries as we
stand by the open grave is to be found in him.''

It is the truth which we find in Jesus which will
free our world from its doubt about God, its despair
about man, its slavery to things, and its fear of death.
''What we find in the historical Jesus,'' says Professor
Glover, ''is a much greater thing than omniscience; it
is that freedom of mind, that activity of intellect, which

we associate with all great characters who launch into the world ideas that emancipate. . . . Where the spirit of Jesus is, there will be liberty, and with it a new spirit of joy and freedom. We do not go into the intellectual problems of our day tied and bound, because Jesus set us free; we know whose we are and whom we serve; we know the type of mind that he loved, the type of mind that he gave; and Jesus will be for us, as for those before us, the Author of Freedom.''

WHAT PLACE JESUS?

"What then shall I do with
Jesus who is called Christ?"
MATTHEW 27 : 22.

WHAT PLACE JESUS?

THE LAST WEEK began with the question, "Who is Jesus?" It ended with the question, "What shall I do with Jesus?" And the answer to this first question then, as it always does, determined the answer to the second question. Pilate's question was answered by the Jewish leaders, by the people, and by himself, on the basis of their final estimate of Jesus. In the eyes of the Jewish leaders, Jesus was an impostor, a blasphemer; a man of power and influence with the people, to be sure, and a man who did some wonderful things which they could not explain; but for all that a dangerous character because he challenged the traditions of the elders and stood in the way of the men who were making profit out of their religion. He was a man whose presence disturbed them, whose keen insight into the deepest realities of religion and life revealed their own sham and hypocrisy, and whose passion for righteousness and justice cut squarely across their graft and greed for gain. They would feel much more comfortable in their hypocrisy and crookedness if he were out of the way. It was not ignorance of the

129

proposal of Jesus which prompted these men to demand his crucifixion. They knew exactly what the acceptance of his way of life would mean for their religion and their other interests. Their answer to Pilate's question was a deliberate answer. They knew what they wanted and why.

The people answered this question out of their ignorance. They had accepted the propaganda of the Jewish leaders at its face value. The man who had been hailed as the deliverer of Israel at the beginning of the week was now looked upon as an impostor, as a man who, if he should have his way, would utterly destroy that traffic in the temple from which most of them gained their living. They demanded the crucifixion of Jesus because they had been led to believe, through their ignorance of the real facts in the case, that he was their enemy. In this ignorance they were undoubtedly sincere. Pilate answered this question out of his indifference. It is true that the final argument of the Jews that if he should release Jesus he would not be Cæsar's friend had its weight, and the political motive played its part in the decision to let the mob have its way with Jesus. But because, in the eyes of Pilate, Jesus was nothing more than a poor deluded visionary and enthusiast, whose life or death was not a matter of consequence either way, he decided to give the people what they wanted. Personally, it did not matter to him what happened to Jesus. He was not deeply interested. So he washed his hands of the whole matter and let it go at that.

This question about placing Jesus had to be answered. The Jewish leaders, the people, and Pilate all had him on their hands. They had to do something about him. All the events of his short career, and all the dramatic incidents of the last week, led to this hour of decision. The throngs which crowded the courts of Pilate's judgment hall, and Pilate himself, were face to face with the inescapable, the inevitable, the unavoidable Christ. And they were faced with an inevitable decision concerning him. The Jewish leaders wanted to place the responsibility for this decision upon the shoulders of Pilate. They wanted the sanction of the state upon their murder so it would not seem quite so cold-blooded. Pilate, unwilling to take this responsibility, tried to throw it back upon the Sanhedrin. When he was reminded that this body had no power to pronounce the death sentence and a hint was dropped that Jesus was from Galilee, Jesus was sent to Herod. Herod "played with him for an hour" and sent him back to Pilate. Only the people did not try to avoid the responsibility of putting Jesus out of the way. They seemed perfectly willing to be fooled. And in the end, both the Jewish leaders and Pilate shifted the blame upon their shoulders.

This inevitable question about placing Jesus was answered in the wrong way. The Jews schemed for the death of one who could have filled the empty forms of their religion with a new life, who could have renewed in their hearts the passion of their great prophets for righteousness, justice, and peace, and who, if he had been received and given a chance, could have "redeemed Israel" and caused her to measure up to her destiny as God's chosen people. They rejected a man in whose veins the choicest blood of their race coursed and who died broken-hearted because he could not save that race. The people gave the final word to crucify their best friend, one who had come to bring God close to them, to deliver them from the bondage of a religion whose burdens had become unbearable, and to lead them into a new and abundant life as children of their Heavenly Father. Pilate allowed an innocent man to be crucified, and with him he crucified his own better self and his future peace of mind. And all these paid the full penalty for their wrong answers. The Jewish leaders and the people whom they had fooled paid a terrible price for their decision. They knew the presence of Jesus was dangerous to their present interests. They did not know the destiny of their nation and the fate of their religion depended upon their decision. The full price which Pilate paid for his decision, we do not know. The imaginations of men have painted him in anguish of soul because he had stained his hands with innocent blood, and trying in vain to wash away those stains. Tradition tells us that he was finally banished from the empire to spend his last days in seclusion and die as a madman.

An adequate answer to the question about placing Jesus was not given until the truth dawned upon men as to who Jesus actually was. This truth came first to the disciples. Their first realization of the tremendous truth about Jesus came when they looked into the empty tomb. They had seen his body carefully wrapped and laid in that tomb. They had seen the great stone placed before the tomb and sealed with the Roman seal. And then, after a period of gloom and night and unspeakable disappointment, they had seen the empty tomb and the place where the body had been. Then came the word of the women, "He is risen!" and finally the appearance of Jesus himself. When Jesus made his first appearance to the disciples, Thomas was not present and refused to believe. Then, after eight days, Jesus came again when Thomas was in the group and so convinced this doubting disciple of his reality that he cried out in words which have become the creed of millions, "My Lord and my God." From this hour there was no question about the place which Jesus had in the minds and hearts of the disciples. For them he was "the Christ, the Son of the living God," and the only Saviour of the world.

When Peter exalted Jesus on the day of Pentecost and said, "Let all the house of Israel therefore know assuredly, that God hath made him both Lord and Christ, this Jesus whom ye crucified," hundreds of the very people who had voted to crucify him when he stood before Pilate were "pricked in their hearts" and cried out, "What shall we do?" It was the conviction that this man whom they had helped to kill was none other than the Son of God himself, and that God had vindicated him by raising him up from the dead, that caused these people to give Jesus the place of Lord in their lives. Paul did not answer the question about placing Jesus, in the right way, until he came to know who Jesus was. When the truth dawned

133

upon the keen intellect and sensitive heart of the greatest of the apostles that this Jesus of Nazareth whose followers he had been persecuting to the death and whose faith he was urging men to renounce was the "Christ of God," that "God had highly exalted him, and gave unto him the name which is above every other name," he was ready to say as a "Hebrew of the Hebrews," and as one who had persecuted the Church, "I count all things to be loss for the excellency of the knowledge of Christ Jesus my Lord." Jesus so absolutely replaced everything else in the life of Paul that he could say, "For me to live is Christ." There was no uncertainty in the minds of the early Christians about Jesus.

Jesus is the most inescapable, inevitable, and unavoidable figure in the world to-day. His presence has followed the race across the centuries and to-day haunts individuals and nations with challenges which they cannot evade. The Jesus of the twentieth century is not the prisoner who stands at the mercy of his enemies, but the Lord of all life before whom the whole world is on trial. He is the Jesus who comes as he came to those first disciples, "the doors being shut," and stands in our midst. In the turmoil of the new awakening in India, E. Stanley Jones has met him and says of him: "This age is face to face with Jesus Christ, and the future of religion seems to be bound up with the question of what we are to think of him and his way of life." On the streets, and in the complex and tragic life of a great American city, Ralph W. Sockman has met him and calls him the "inescapable Galilean," saying of him, "He cannot be kept out of any situation. . . . The principles which Christ revealed are as inescapable as the principles revealed by the falling stone. The doors of a situation can no more be locked against his laws than they can be locked against the laws of gravity." A poet, Harry Kemp, puts the tremendous fact of the inescapable Christ into these fine verses:

"I cannot put his presence by, I meet him everywhere.
I meet him in the country town, the busy market square:
The mansion and the tenement attest his presence there.

Upon the funneled ships at sea he sets his shining feet:
The distant ends of empire not in vain his name repeat:
And like the presence of a rose, he makes the whole world sweet.

He comes to break the barriers down raised up by barren creeds;
About the globe from zone to zone, like sunlight, he proceeds.
He comes to give the world's starved heart the perfect love it
    needs—

The Christ whose friends have played him false, whom dogmas
    have belied,
Still speaking to the hearts of men—though shamed and cru-
    cified,
The Master of the centuries, who will not be denied."

This inevitable Christ will be faced and placed to-day according to what men think of him. There is no greater fallacy than that which leads us to suppose that it makes very little difference what the world

135

thinks about Jesus Christ so far as its actual life is concerned. It makes all the difference between a pagan and a Christian civilization. The real values of our civilization must ever be measured in terms of the final estimate which men place upon the character of Jesus Christ. Those who look upon him and his message as a disturbing element in our modern life will want to get rid of him. When men know that Jesus' evaluation of human life is right, that the individual is worth more than the whole material universe and every human body is the temple of an immortal soul, they cannot go on treating their fellows like "hands" and "tools" and feel very comfortable about it. When the war-makers recognize Jesus' philosophy of love as the greatest enemy of the war system, they will want to get Jesus out of the way. All of those powerful interests which are openly unfriendly toward Jesus and his Church and who would like to have the influence of religion reduced to a mere shadow take this attitude because they know Jesus stands squarely in the way of their selfish interests. They have evaluated him in terms of their own selfishness and do not want him around.

Great masses of people in our modern world either give Jesus no place at all in their lives or become the easy victims of those selfish interests who are trying to eliminate him. Thousands of people who are loyal to the Church as an organization and to the outward forms of religion are ignorant of the real significance of Jesus for our modern life. They accept, and peddle on the streets and in their homes, and sometimes even

136

in the Church, all sorts of propaganda which cuts squarely across the fundamental ideals of the teachings of Jesus. Thousands of members of the Church vote against Jesus, vote to crucify him over and over again, without being aware of what they are doing. And in our modern life there are many people for whom life no longer has any spiritual values, who are utterly indifferent about the fate of Jesus. This is the attitude which prevails to an alarming extent in many of our outstanding educational institutions. Jesus and his way of living are not even mentioned, except by way of ridicule, in the list of values which comes from hundreds of classrooms. Jesus is so absolutely insignificant in the eyes of a whole group of our modern intellectuals that what the world does with him and his Church is not a matter of any concern at all. They wash their hands of the whole matter of religion and just leave it at that. For them, all the values in life which we have associated with Jesus and his religion are mere fictions or illusions. Jesus is being placed in the twentieth century on the basis of what men think of him and his message.

Forty years ago, in a sermon based upon the question of Pilate, an American preacher said: "What to do with Christ is the question of the ages. It is the master question of our generation. God seems in these latter days to be tightening his grip on the reins of human affairs, and to be driving the race with the swiftness of judgment to choose between the kingdom of Christ or no government at all; between the absolute reign of Christ and the anarchy of absolute atheism. Though the world may try to evade the real issue, try to shut its eyes to the divine signals, try to halt between Mammon and Christ, yet the inevitable issue of the swiftly converging crises of history will be the acceptance of Christ's law of love, or the triumph of the world spirit of selfishness with its universal confusion and violence.'' The world made the choice between Christ and atheism—a practical atheism which caused men to go through the motions of worshiping God in their beautiful churches and at the same time living just as if there were no God; an atheism which put Mammon upon the throne, substituted force for love and ill will and suspicion for good will and brotherhood. The world shut its eyes to the ''divine signals'' and plunged into the night of war and the darker night which has followed. Could any terms be more descriptive of what has prevailed on the face of the earth since August, 1914, and that which stares us in the face for the future than ''universal confusion and violence''?

Will we make the same mistake again? Jesus and Mammon are both bidding for first place. The nineteenth century and the first decade of the twentieth century witnessed the nations in a mad scramble for material possessions and power. Jesus Christ was cast aside and the ethical and social implications of his religion were ignored even by the majority of the leaders in his Church. In many cases the Church became the mouthpiece for an order of things which was based upon principles directly opposed to the message of Jesus. At the close of the World War an American

138

newspaper editor summed up the results of it all in these words: "The climax of it all was the World War. That was the culmination and destination of materiality. Grasping hands reached out for loot and met clinched fists. It was the final test of an effort to ignore divine teaching. And now the world sits in sodden dismay—sits in desolation in fields that are drenched with blood and slaughter and tears—sits wondering from what direction can come a single ray of hope. . . . Well, we have tried the other way. The diplomats and the marching armies and the greedy fingers tried the other way. And beaten to our knees, breathless, heartsick, and afraid, the shattered world asks itself the question, 'What is the way out of this wilderness of desolation and sorrow?' "

In that hour did the Church of Jesus Christ come forward with an adequate answer to this question? Did it make the way so clear and so unmistakable that the world was ready to walk in that way? It did not. While the world was on its knees waiting for some answer to the deepest cry of its heart, the Church was doing something else. Here in America, at least, the churches reverted to an orgy of inflation and expansion and denominational rivalry and controversy. The Inter-Church World Movement went to pieces on the rocks of a selfish denominationalism, and following that the religious air was filled with the dust of innumerable conflicts within the life of the great religious bodies. Conventions and general assemblies reminded one of the western front with Modernists and Fundamentalists intrenched on either side and a few peace-

139

makers struggling in vain in no man's land to call the Church back to its fundamental task. While the world waited for the Christ who is "the way, the truth, and the life," the Church which had been intrusted with his message was strangely silent. The great message of the Church was sidetracked to make way for the religious promoters and politicians. And out of many of our colleges and universities there came an apologetic attitude toward Jesus Christ which was reflected in an utterly negative message from hundreds of pulpits. Neither the Jesus of the Modernists nor the Jesus of the Fundamentalists has been sufficient to answer the world's question. The bubble of all our mighty promotional schemes has burst in the face of the leaders of the Church. The world has turned away from a Jesus who is only human, or who may or may not have lived at all but still remains as a beautiful ideal, as being too unreal. It has refused to be satisfied with a Jesus who is coming some day on the clouds of glory, but who is not interested in what men are suffering here and now. It has been bored and disgusted by the insistent demands of the promoters.

What has been the result of this failure of the Church? Instead of going forward into a new order of things the world went back into the same old way and entered upon the wildest orgy of materialism that history has yet recorded. Men went back to another mad scramble for material things. In Europe the nations went back to the same old business of building up huge armies and navies and preparing for another war. The only hope for the future lies in Jesus Christ.

140

Until he is given his rightful place in the lives of men and nations there can be no salvation for our civilization. It is not a trite saying, but one of the most sober facts of our modern life, that it is "Christ or chaos." Every other way has proven to be futile.

Before Jesus is given his rightful place in the life of our age, two things must happen. There must be a crusade of preaching which will make Jesus just as real to men as the preaching of the first Christians did; and room must be made for him in the hearts of individual men. Until men take Jesus Christ seriously as the Son of God, as one who has the right to make certain demands upon their lives in the name of God, they will not be concerned about giving him any place of importance in the affairs of this world. And Jesus will never change our civilization until he has first changed the hearts of men. He asked while he was on earth, first of all, for a place in the hearts of men, knowing full well that if he could reign there he could reign in every realm of human society. The task of making individual Christians cannot be neglected for the seemingly larger task of making a Christian world. The social emphasis, the evangelistic program, and the educational task of the Church are one. The only Christian order Jesus knew anything about was that order which was to come through Christianized individuals. We have been impatient of this method because it is slow. But Jesus never promised that the kingdom would come overnight. When we have tried to force its growth or to take it by violence, we have always failed.

141

Dr. S. Parkes Cadman, who surely could not be accused of underestimating the social message of Christianity, spoke wisely when he said: "Despite the generalizing of some visionaries to-day, Christianity begins with the individual soul. Jesus staked the future of his mission, not on the mass, but on twelve selected men. Although he anticipated world conquest, he founded his anticipation on love, not force or diplomacy, and on love operative in every single heart. It seemed ridiculous to the imperial thinkers of his time that a faith which originated so modestly and defied the counsels of their wisdom should prosper. . . . But it did prosper, and its triumphs are a part of the history of the race for the past two thousand years, and by far the noblest part at that. . . . In the words of the Bible, it is not by might nor by power that civilization is to be redeemed, but by the indwelling, saving, restoring, renewing Spirit of the living God." All schemes for the redemption of the world are doomed to failure until Jesus is given first place in the hearts of men.

The Cure for a Troubled heart

The Disciples were troubled. Jesus was going away.

1 Belief in God
2 Belief in Jesus
3 Belief in the fathers house